What's the Big Idea?
34 Ideas for a Better Australia

First published in 2025 by Australia Institute Press

The Australia Institute
australiainstitute.org.au

Copyright © in the individual pieces remains with the authors 2025

All rights reserved. Without limiting the rights under copyright below, no part of this publication shall be reproduced, stored in or introduced into a retrieval system, or transmitted in any form or by any means (electronic, mechanical, photocopying, recording or otherwise), without the prior permission of both the copyright holder and the publisher. The moral rights of the authors have been asserted in accordance with the Copyright, Designs and Patents Act 1988 in Australia, and the Copyright Act 1994 in New Zealand.

978-1-7636621-0-0 (hardback)
9781-7-636621-2-4 (paperback)
978-1-7438240-6-1 (digital)

Cover and internal design and typesetting copyright © Australia Institute Press 2025
Proofread by Rod Morrison
Cataloguing-in-publication data is available from the National Library of Australia

What's the Big Idea?
34 Ideas for a Better Australia

Edited by Anna Chang and Alice Grundy

Australia
Institute
→ Press

Contents

Editors' Note 1

Foreword: When Relaxed and Comfortable Doesn't Cut It. 5
John McKinnon

Introduction: The Australia Institute — 30 Years On. 9
The Hon Michael Kirby AC CMG

Why Australians Must Shed the Fear of a Larger State 21
Yanis Varoufakis

After the Voice Referendum There are Two Paths 25
Pat Anderson AO

Free Her Speech: Violence Against Women and
Anti-SLAPP Laws for Australia. 33
Jennifer Robinson

Action for Green Transformation Needs Politics of Inclusion 39
Sunita Narain

Culture, Money and Morals. 43
Louise Adler AM

Destination Disaster: The Urgent Call from the
Pacific Island People. 49
His Excellency Anote Tong

First Nations Powering the Energy Transition. 53
Karrina Nolan

The Democratisation of Data for Improving Child and
Family Health and Wellbeing 59
Professor Fiona Stanley AC and Associate Professor Rebecca Glauert

If Australia Could Be Brave 65
Amy Remeikis

Understanding What We Are Up Against 69
Thomas Mayo

Three Things You Need to Know About Climate Change 75
Dr Joëlle Gergis

A Radical Act of Diplomacy 81
Professor Clare Wright OAM

Frameworks of Insecurity 87
President José Ramos-Horta

National Power, Agency and a Foreign Policy that Delivers 95
Allan Behm

In Defence of Public Broadcasting 99
Alex Sloan AM

Doing Politics Differently: Safeguarding Australian Democracy . . . 103
Alana Johnson AM

The Concrete Language of a Dying Planet 107
Anna Spargo-Ryan

Worker Voice 111
Sally McManus

How to Plan Cities for Climate Change 115
Lucy Hughes Turnbull AO

The Right Kind of Action: Tackling the Housing Crisis 121
Maiy Azize

Proportional Representation:
The Key to Restoring Democracy 125
Christine Milne AO

Truth, Transparency and Whistleblowing:
The Case for a Federal Whistleblower Protection Authority 131
Kieran Pender

No Backbone 137
Dr Richard Denniss

The Mental Health Crisis and Solutions 143
Professor Patrick McGorry AO

Wage Growth is Good 151
Greg Jericho

The Price of Extinction 157
Bob Brown

Democratic Solidarity 161
Dr Emma Shortis

An Australian Peace and Security Strategy 165
Professor John Langmore AM

Caution is Killing Us 171
Polly Hemming

Confronting Reality in an Evolving Information and Communications
Mediascape 177
Professor Peter Doherty AC

Politics is Good 181
Bill Browne

Australia's Role in Ridding the World of Nuclear Weapons 185
Hon Melissa Parke

Curiosity-driven Research 191
Professor Brian Schmidt AC

Afterword 197
Dr Richard Denniss

Contributor Biographies 203
Acknowledgements 215

Editors' Note

When we first sat down to talk about how The Australia Institute could commemorate our 30th anniversary, what came to mind was how much the Institute had grown. Over the last 30 years, certainly, but also during our respective tenures at the Institute, there has been incredible change for both the organisation and for Australia as a country. Things that we once thought impossible are possible, and ideas that once seemed radical are now part of the mainstream. We recall thinking, "Can we even say that?" about ideas that have grown wings and taken flight. That's the work of a think tank, and that's what intellectual leadership looks like.

Since The Australia Institute launched in 1994, so many ideas and research initiated under the letterhead have either changed the nature of the public policy debate in Australia or even changed policy. While much has changed over the last 30 years, our charitable purpose — to create a more just, peaceful and sustainable society — remains the same. And at a time of catastrophic climate change, mass extinction, record company profits, growing inequality, and the erosion of the foundations of democracies around the world, it is hard to think of a time where there has been a greater need for big thinking to tackle the enormity of the problems we face.

When we considered how we could bring together or create a lasting record of the amazing friends The Australia Institute has made over the past three decades — some of Australia and the world's leading thinkers — the idea for this book was formed.

As we began collating lists of the incredible people who have been so generous to lend their time and their names to all manner of Australia Institute open letters, webinars, reports and events, what struck us was what all these people had in common: the boldness of their thinking, and the unifying idea that the solutions to our biggest problems were within our grasp, if only we as a nation had the mettle to reach for them.

We set out to publish a collection of 30 essays to commemorate 30 years of big ideas at The Australia Institute, but the response exceeded our expectations, and here in your hands are 34 big ideas for a better Australia.

Following on from the 2023 Voice Referendum, Aunty Pat Anderson and Thomas Mayo offer some reflections and ideas for the path forward. Clare Wright describes the extraordinary potential embodied in the Yirrkala Bark Petitions. Polly Hemming, Louise Adler and Amy Remeikis call on Australians to be brave as we face the biggest crises in the history of humankind.

Brian Schmidt reflects on the role of curiosity-driven research and Kieran Pender and Jennifer Robinson offer ways that changes to Australian law can improve conditions for whistleblowers and women reporting sexual assaults. Alex Sloan writes on the importance of the public broadcaster and Peter Doherty emphasises the importance of access to accurate and comprehensible information for citizens and lawmakers alike.

Despite being a wealthy country, there are significant shortfalls in health policy to which Fiona Stanley, Rebecca Glauert and Patrick McGorry offer solutions. Christine Milne, Bill Browne and Alana Johnson reflect on what is working and what is not in Australian democratic processes. Looking beyond our shores, Emma Shortis, John Langmore and Allan Behm ask what role Australia can choose to play on the world stage, and Melissa Parke shows the shortcomings in current approaches to nuclear weapons. President José Ramos-Horta explores what the word "security" actually means in the context of international relations.

As the climate crisis intensifies, Sunita Narain and Anote Tong write about the massive discrepancies in the effects of climate change on different communities. Joëlle Gergis relates three things you need to know about climate change and Anna Spargo-Ryan addresses the need for concrete language when describing the crisis we face.

Bob Brown, Richard Denniss and Yanis Varoufakis ask us to reassess how we think about the economy and its relationship to society, while Sally McManus and Greg Jericho think through the future of workers. Lucy Hughes Turnbull and Karrina Nolan consider the ways planning and construction in cities and in First Nations communities can make for more comfortable conditions as the planet warms, while Maiy Azize contributes to the debate on how we can address housing shortages.

Just as the contributions to this book are bold and wide-ranging, Michael Kirby's introduction reminds us of the boldness in the hope of what The Australia Institute would become when he launched the Institute all those years ago. He highlights how diverse the research impact of the Institute has been and continues to be. John McKinnon's foreword reminds us that aiming for relaxed and comfortable is not defensible and that the work of the Institute is pushing for far more positive change.

We hope that what you take away from this book is the proof that big problems can be solved, and many solutions are within our reach. Australia matters, and here in your hands is a collection of ideas for how we can make a better Australia together.

Foreword:
When Relaxed and Comfortable Doesn't Cut It

John McKinnon

Thirty years old. It certainly is an achievement to celebrate but also a time to reflect on why The Australia Institute exists and why we need to push on towards another 30 years.

Thirty years ago, Australia was experiencing the final years of the Hawke–Keating era. That period, from 1983 to 1996, was a time of significant economic and structural reform, and of new visions of who Australia was as a country and how we relate to the rest of the world, and our close neighbours in particular.

That era ended in 1996 with the election of the Howard government. John Howard detected a tiredness in the Australian people and took to the election a vision of being "relaxed and comfortable". The era of big-picture reform was over (at least rhetorically) and the time had come to slow the pace, accept the status quo and maybe just tinker around the edges. Despite the fact that Howard's government did implement some big reforms (think GST and

WorkChoices), the idea of government as managers, rather than reformers, took hold.

Since that time, parties have fought elections on a "small target strategy". The perceived lessons of the 1993 "Fightback!" election were only reinforced in 2019 when Bill Shorten proposed a series of modest tax proposals and lost the election. Rightly or wrongly, accepted wisdom came to consider bold policy proposals electoral liabilities.

In such an electoral climate, the inequality that arose from the neoliberal reforms of the 1980s became entrenched and progressive change considered near impossible. Conversely, as that inequality grew and became entrenched, progressive change was never more necessary. "Relaxed and comfortable" was no longer an appropriate modus operandi. It was in such a climate that The Australia Institute came into being, grew and thrived.

Over that 30 years, the Institute has filled the gap left by an increasingly politicised public service and timid political class. The Institute has taken up the bold ideas, backed them with rigorous research and promoted the results into the public square. In doing so, it has proven the accepted wisdom wrong. Progressive change is not only possible, but usually popular.

In filling this gap, I consider The Australia Institute has become an essential and vital component of Australia's democracy. Democracy works when there is a true contest of ideas, competing visions of our nation's future and rigorously researched arguments for each case that are put to the public in language they can understand.

As we look forward to the next 30 years, our vantage point is unrecognisable compared to that of 1994. The challenges of the future, be they climate change, geopolitics or democracy itself, loom large, if not insurmountable. We face them, however, knowing we have an institution up to the task. If the past 30 years involved The Australia Institute growing to fill a gap, the next 30 will involve The Australia Institute applying those same values to lead the way to that fairer and more equitable society we all desire.

Introduction: The Australia Institute — 30 Years On

The Hon Michael Kirby AC CMG

Trash fights back

I join the celebration of the 30th anniversary of The Australia Institute. Long ago, in its first decade, I had two significant engagements with the Institute. The first was on 4 May 1994 when I spoke at its launch in Canberra. The second was on 10 May 2000, also in Canberra, when I joined in the opening of new offices at the Australian National University. In a sense, like Dean Acheson and the United Nations, I was present at the creation.

In 1994, without a great deal of knowledge of what was expected of the new Institute, I pushed it forward upon an unsuspecting nation. Oddly — as I reflect — I chose as my theme: "Trash Fights Back". A few days before the launch, I had received a letter from a "Mrs M.W.", described as a disgruntled citizen from

Victoria. She had written complaining about the plight of persons like herself, with high talent but unemployed: one of the "new poor". She explained that "the official level of unemployment in Australia had stood for some time at 11%". She declared that "Australia cannot *trash* such a large pool of talent, skill, hard-work and commitment, without devastating long-term consequences. Nor can those who 'have', avert their gaze from this challenge any longer, without guilt. It could, and might, be them."

Looking back with today's eyes, the high level of unemployment at the time the Institute was created does seem pretty intolerable. It was unsurprising that a new institute, which boldly took its title as "*The Australia* Institute", should start by addressing the problem of endemic unemployment. One of the directors of the new institute, Emeritus Professor John Nevile, claimed that there was a "general consensus among economists" that, based on the experience of the late 1970s and 1980s, nothing significant was about to happen to reduce the then current unemployment levels in Australia. Without the achievement of a national growth rate above 3.5% and possibly the development of a "new manufacturing sector", nothing hopeful could really be expected. According to Professor Nevile, writing in the 1990s:

> The character of unemployment has changed. The long-term unemployed are not likely to get jobs even in the hoped-for boom for the rest of the decade. These conditions totally undercut [expert] forecasts as well as [their] philosophical emphasis on "job readiness" for jobs that do not exist.

At the time of the launch of The Australia Institute, I was serving as President of the Court of Appeal of New South Wales after a decade as Chairman of the Australian Law Reform Commission;

I had recently also been appointed by the World Health Organization in Geneva as a Commissioner of the new Global Commission on AIDS. I was gradually becoming more involved in the global movement to address the HIV/AIDS pandemic. My attempt to emphasise new strategies for engaging with LGBT minorities, drug users, sex workers, and others in the frontline of exposure to the human immunodeficiency virus (HIV) was a big ask. It led to my being attacked for standing up for human "trash".

Lee Kuan Yew had recently boasted of the success of Singapore's hardline policies on "trash" in the population. He warned Australians that unless they energetically punished all of the groups with whom I wanted to engage, these people would turn Australia into the "white trash of Asia". I was rather recalcitrant about these dire predictions and the remedies that Mr Lee — a very intelligent man — was pedalling for us. For him the solution to all our woes was to rediscover the "work ethic"; and to diminish the power of "bloody-minded unions protecting unproductive work practices, feather bedding and inflexibility in wages".

In my remarks, on the other hand, I urged that the attention of the Institute should rather be addressed to increasing the equal role of women in the economy; giving "high priority to the process of reconciliation with the Aboriginal and Torres Strait Islander people" facing multiple disadvantages in Australia; and "changing the laws on sexual minorities, drug use, and consensual adult same-sex practices". Only in these ways, I suggested, could Australia really become the land of the "fair go" that it endlessly praised itself as being.

Looking back, my launch speech for the Institute contended that the way forward needed to offer appropriate emphasis on economic reform; but also to social reform, that was interconnected. Each of these strategies was intrinsically joined to the other.

To those in Australian society, at that time, who suggested that the all-powerful priority for the new institute should be economic reform, I offered a splash of cold water. Economics was very important, but it was not, I contended, everything.

> [W]hat I hope [for] this institute [is that it] will tell governments in Australia, of all persuasions, oppositions, universities and citizens ... the self-evident truth: [that] economics is not all. There are vital social and spiritual values which must mollify the operation of the market. It will be for the Institute to develop this self-evident verity into practical policies — backed up by sound research and hard thinking. I believe that all of the political parties in Australia thirst for a better way ahead, to assure the restoration of the "fair go" society in Australia. So, let us answer Mrs M.W. ... We are determined not to "trash" you. We have a new Australian resolve and a new Australia Institute which will play its part to restore meaning and definition to the lives of those whom the economic rationalists have effectively discarded to a "trash" heap of economically hopeless cases. The unemployed are not "trash" whom we must pay fortnightly to preserve their silence and not to upset too much the "haves" and those who worship at the altar of a proud economic imperium.

Rationality and constitutionalism

By the year 2000, when we celebrated the move of the offices of the Institute in Canberra, I had been appointed a Justice of the High Court of Australia, housed on the other side of Lake Burley Griffin. Not irretrievably put off by my message on the occasion of the establishment of the Institute, I was asked to come on 10 May 2000 to help launch its new premises. It was an event celebrated at University House at the ANU.

On this occasion, I had to be more circumspect in what I said. I reminded my listeners of my need to avoid expression of any views, however banal, on issues that, directly or indirectly, might come before the High Court. On any such issues, extreme prudence was the rule for me, so that I was not later disqualified from expressing my opinion in my new institution where "my views can actually count".

Nevertheless, encouraged by the early experiences of the Institute, and my earlier decade chairing the Australian Law Reform Commission, I urged its participants to continue playing a useful role "as an organ of analysis, data gathering and exposition". These tasks were, in my view, a vital contribution to the effective operation of the democracy for which the Australian Constitution provided, then nearing the celebration of its own first century.

By 2000 there were far more "think tanks" in Australia. Many of them were dependent on private funding. Some of them were overtly partisan. Many were inclined to see issues through the perspective of a conservative, rather than a liberal, viewpoint. Obviously, such viewpoints are legitimate in a democracy. Neither side of the spectrum of opinion could enjoy permanent supremacy. All should compete to contribute to the mixture of research, experience and opinion: offering reasoned solutions to national and international economic and social challenges and controversies. Unless this was achieved, the result would be depressing for The Australia Institute and the nation that the Institute claimed to assess and cajole.

The alternative is what we see so often in Australia and, indeed, throughout the Western world. It is government by transient political polling, newspaper headlines and editorials and media creations — the pursuit of "issues" as a form of mass entertainment.

Thoughtful and informed criticisms are often missing as we lurch from one issue, abstracted from the news, blown up out of all proportion, popularised and sensationalised, until it too is replaced by the next storm [released for] the entertainment of the people. All political parties are victims and participants in this feature of modern democratic government. Governance too easily falls victim to populism. I do not believe that this is the kind of democratic polity that the founders of the Australian Constitution envisaged when they finalised the document, 100 years ago.

There are some media outlets that I will not name — although everyone knows who they are — that have been intolerant towards the approaches sometimes taken by The Australia Institute. Inferentially, this has been so because the Institute refused to conform to their world view of where our country is, and where it should be headed.

The Institute had advocated solutions to national and global problems in the economy and in society that look similar to those offered by the left side of politics. The Institute was attacked for proclaiming that its commitment was to avoid party political entanglements. Some observers complained that The Australia Institute was too uniformly favourable to a liberal or leftist approach.

However, what I said in 2000 in my view remains true today:

> The Australia Institute and other such bodies offer an alternative vision of democracy. This is the democracy of ideas, of objective data, of strongly stressed opinions and arguments, of practical philosophy, of strong persuasion. We need more of this from every political viewpoint and philosophy ... Sometimes we will object to the views expressed [by the Institute]. Sometimes we will disagree. Occasionally, we will be irritated and once or twice infuriated. That is precisely

what The Australia Institute is here for. That is democracy as our constitution guarantees it. Freedom lies in difference. Not in sameness. In disagreement, not in cloying consensus. I hope that The Australia Institute will never forget that stimulation and irritation are part of its mission.

The attributes that I singled out at the beginning of the present century are also vital for universities and other places of research and scholarship. They are vital for the courts and for the apolitical branches of government. Avoidance of political partisanship and an even commitment to sound research and principled decision-making are proclaimed ideals of the Australian political system. In practical politics, such ideas are sometimes overlooked or ignored. Recent instances in the United States show what can happen when political partisanship intrudes illegitimately into universities, the courts, and the highest levels of the public service. Those who watched the political campaigns waged in the 2024 US presidential election will be aware of the same sharp divisions of partisanship. It is not entirely different in Australia.

So, has The Australia Institute adhered to the aspirations that I collected on its launch? On occasion, being a human institution, it has, no doubt, failed to uphold the aspirations that those who founded and established it embraced and declared as their own. What does the scorecard tell us about the Institute 30 years on?

Achievements and challenges

If the overall purpose of The Australia Institute, from its inception, was to contribute to a just, peaceful, sustainable Australia — and thereby to a just, peaceful and sustainable world — what have been the foremost achievements in the past 30 years? What are the challenges that still lie ahead?

Today, the Institute is commonly focused on conducting research that matters: research that is timely and useful to Australian society and its governance. Research that can be reported widely and understood by citizens. It is not enough for the Institute to be simply a contrary or alternative voice to the status quo. In the early days, the goal was to hold a mirror up to Australian society. At that time there were not many progressive voices and ideas reaching the mainstream. This was the environment in which the Institute aimed to offer its alternative voice. There was a void calling for reforms that were highly challenging to the mainstream of influential opinion. Fresh opinions challenged the then unquestioning zeal towards privatisation. The Institute called out the defects and occasional injustices of neoliberalism. It identified the important role of Australia as a major cause of climate change; and consequently laid emphasis on our obligation to adopt and persevere with beneficial, sometimes unpopular, responses.

The Institute had boldly set out to change the course of Australia. However, in very real ways, the nation had actually caught up with many of the aspirations of the Institute. The Institute has played a successful part in leading many debates and fostering new policy ideas. Meanwhile, the country has shifted its goals and policies. Ideas that were radical in their time, including talk about improving the environment; reducing inequality; and protecting Indigenous and other vulnerable minorities, are all now mainstream. The advances continue to gather pace and to afford new opportunities to The Australia Institute to offer new and powerful ideas as to what kind of country Australia is and should become.

Australia matters. What we do as a nation matters accordingly. If we believe in democracy, we must also believe in politics and its capacity to be the instrument of progress and change. It is necessary to embrace the conviction that serious problems can ultimately be fixed. That we are not helpless onlookers who simply observe the defects of our society. We need, for example, to proclaim that tax is not an evil. That it has the potential to be a significant good in our society. Tax is the price we all pay for living together in a civilised, safe and peaceful society.

At the turn of the 19th century, on the brink of the 20th century, academic opinion embraced the view that two young nations would ride the tide that had swelled as European empires started to fade. The inheritors of the old imperial era were often named as Australia and Argentina. Since this perception, Australia has embraced much change. But it has continued to operate on an uncorrupted and universal system of taxation. With some exceptions, the overwhelming majority of Australians pay their taxes. Often tax is deducted at the source, as became our practice during Australia's existential crisis in World War II. However, Argentina was a different story.

In Argentina the system of taxation lost its universal application. The wealthy could evade the obligation to pay tax. The burdens of taxation fell most heavily on the poor. For the wealthy, it was all too often optional; and readily evaded.

The Australia Institute does not shy away from engaging in political debates. The Institute embraces and seeks to sustain democracy. It views its work as vital to producing a better and more informed democratic debate for beneficial outcomes supported by democratic institutions. The challenges to which the work of The Australia Institute has contributed, over the 30 years since its creation, have been wide-ranging.

A fairer approach to income tax cuts. The federal government in 2024 announced changes to the Stage 3 tax cuts. It delivered an additional $84 billion to low- and middle-income earners over 10 years. This shift was influenced by five years of research and analysis by The Australia Institute. It was considered mission impossible, until it happened.

Challenging consensus on profit and inflation. The Institute's research delivered outcomes that argued corporate profits, not wages, were driving inflation. This has challenged one of the sacred tenets of Australian economic management. It has contributed to pushback from the strategies energetically urged by some officials of the federal Treasury, some pro-business media outlets and lobby groups, and many politicians.

The Institute has persistently supported, and provided data to support, a national anti-corruption institution. The fate of Argentina and countries like it must ever remain a warning for us of what happens when illegality and corruption replace integrity and the rule of law. This can be demonstrated by global and national data and research. And research has always been the core business of the Institute.

Over 30 years, The Australia Institute has generated social data that helps to define Australia's role in causing climate change. This includes data that indicates Australia is one of the biggest emitters of the active agents that cause climate change. We are the world's third-largest fossil fuel exporter. We provide $14 billion a year in fossil fuel subsidies. We pay to fossil fuel companies more, in sustenance and governmental support, than Australia contributes in international aid to Pacific islands and other neighbours. Yet our neighbours face urgent existential dangers, seemingly tolerated by us so that we can live in the sunshine.

The Australia Institute's program recently has been wide-ranging and includes a host of public events. In 2024 the Institute conducted a national tour on inequality with Executive Director Richard Denniss and a national tour with Nobel Laureate Joseph Stiglitz. In 2024, the Institute hosted President José Ramos-Horta of Timor-Leste who spoke at the Sydney Opera House on the topic of Australia's security relationship with Timor-Leste and labour mobility. Professor Allan Fels and Sally McManus offered the Laurie Carmichael Oration on the role of profits in driving inflation.

Recently, the Institute has released a wide range of research on issues and problems as diverse as companies using blood tests for screening potential workers; the rapid rise of wealth inequality; civic education and its role in a democracy; the amount of Australian gas surrendered to multinational companies without charge; the inequality and inefficiency of exempting large 4WD vehicles from luxury car tax; trends in Australian voting patterns and the consequences of the rising number of independent members of Parliament and minor parties in Australian parliaments; and the importance of worker voices in workplaces and the consequential need for legal protections for their union representatives who lift their voices.

Just as economic issues are not the only ones that deserve the vigilant scrutiny of The Australia Institute, so other social and individual challenges require its attention. A research institution that has adopted the name of "The Australia Institute" must never think small. Its title and aspirations require it to think big. It must aspire to a significant and growing national role that assists our democracy to reach its optimum potential. It travels beyond slogans and political catchcries and superficial politics. By embracing statistics, rigorous scrutiny, public discussion and sound analysis, the Institute must access and exhibit the aspiration to stimulate our democracy. In the process, it will take risks that may upset some timorous souls. The Australia Institute must ever be a place for bold spirits.

Why Australians Must Shed the Fear of a Larger State

Yanis Varoufakis

Three are the most dangerous fantasies that Australia labours under. The first is that only the private sector innovates. The second is that all wealth is produced by privateers before it is collectivised by the state through the tax system. And the third is that public debt is worse than private debt. Taken together, these three fantasies have convinced most Australians that the state can never be too small — a conviction that poses a real and present threat to Australia's future.

To get a feel for this, hold your smartphone in your hand and recall how the likes of Apple, Samsung, Sony, Microsoft and so on portray these devices as the epitome of capitalist innovation made possible by their brilliant engineers. However, were you to take it apart (not recommended!), you would end up with components (microchips, touch screen, battery), each of which was invented either in some state laboratory or on the strength of some government grant.

Now, consider one of your phone's or tablet's or laptop's most useful features: its wi-fi device which was invented in Australia by badly paid researchers employed by the underfunded state-owned

CSIRO (in association with another public institution, Macquarie University). And ask yourself the question: could a private Australian company have invented, patented and made such a device function? While miracles never cease, only a research centre like the CSIRO, together with a public university, could have realistically offered America's Big Tech a great gift like wi-fi.

And, yet, the Australian public remains largely oblivious to this, ready and willing to go along with any populist who offers tax cuts funded by cuts to organisations like the CSIRO, which are uniquely placed to help Australian engineers participate in the digital revolution — without having to move to San Francisco or to Shanghai, that is. As a result, stellar state organisations like the CSIRO remain underfunded and left to their own devices.

Reprehensively, even after inventing something as special as wi-fi, the Australian Government lent little assistance when the CSIRO sought to claw back some of the profits Big Tech had made by seizing upon its wi-fi invention. It would not be too controversial to say that the Australian Government seemed keener to appease the privateers of America's Big Tech than to ensure that its own CSIRO was rewarded fairly and, thus, empowered to make Australia's next contribution to the digital or biotech revolution.

Why are our politicians behaving in this way? How come we do not punish them at the polling booths for aiding and abetting another country's Big Tech against our own venerable institutions? The sad answer is: it does not occur to the wider Australian public that their state *can* innovate, and that the scientists and experts it keeps from migrating to distant lands *do* create value that does not come from some hole in the ground.

To change the public's mindset, so that Australian governments are compelled by public opinion to support homegrown innovation, it is not enough to remind the public that the Australian state has been a great innovator in the past (for example: hydroelectric power, laying down railway tracks and electricity grids that the private sector would never build). We need also to help our fellow Australians escape the double trap of thinking that the state is a drag on development and that public debt is the worst of all evils.

Let us begin with the toxic illusion that less public debt is *always* good for an economy's dynamism. Austerians peddle public deficit phobia mainly because they want to scare the public off spending money on those who need it (including the poor who are also disabled, elderly or young) while sparing no expense when it comes to subsidising those who do not need it (such as the fossil fuel barons, private schools and arms dealers). In the process, the central belief they successfully implant in the majority's collective mind, that governments must do whatever it takes to slash public debt (to zero, if possible), depletes the state's capacity to produce the wealth that can drive shared prosperity.

Somewhere around this point I can sense my austerian critics jumping at the opportunity to highlight my other nationality (Greek), and my brief tenure as the finance minister of the most bankrupt European state, to say: "How typical of this Greek to lure us Australians into his debt trap" — to which I shall reply by reminding them that I only agreed to take on Greece's finance ministry in order to prevent the Greek state taking on more public debt because, yes, there is such a thing as too much crippling public debt. The point I am making here, however, is that Australia is facing the opposite danger: not enough investment due to a debilitating public-debt phobia.

To see this, forget Greece (an unhelpful analogy for Australia) and turn, instead, to Singapore (a truly instructive example for Australians). Singapore's public debt, as a proportion of national income, is seven and a half times that of Australia's. Is this evidence that the Australian state is leaner and fitter than Singapore's? Absolutely not. In fact, Singapore's government budget is, on average, in surplus — unlike Australia's. So, how come Singapore has a debt to income ratio of 168% compared to the Australian Commonwealth's 22%?

It's simple: Singapore's state borrows huge amounts of money every year not to pay for its running costs, salaries, state benefits, armaments and so on (recall that it runs a budget surplus) but on behalf of state-owned investment and social wealth funds (like Temasek) which, in turn, invest in start-ups, social housing, foreign enterprises and, yes, CSIRO-like homegrown innovative organisations that repay in kind with high quality jobs, high spending power and massive long-term social returns. In other words, exactly what the Australian Government is loath to do under the spell of austerians inflicting a great deal of damage to this country by instilling, through complicit media, a public-deficit phobia and an ill-considered antipathy to the state.

After the Voice Referendum There are Two Paths

Pat Anderson AO

On the evening of 14 October 2023, I was watching the results of the Referendum come in with a group of Uluru Dialogue activists and their friends and family in Brisbane. We had spent the day travelling around polling booths in Logan on the outskirts of the city, supporting the local volunteers and asking people to vote in favour of establishing the First Nations Voice to Parliament.

We knew the polls had turned against us.

Initially, after the 2017 Uluru Statement from the Heart called for the establishment of the Voice, Australia's people were strongly behind us. The ABC's Vote Compass in April 2022 found almost three-quarters of respondents supported "an amendment to the constitution to establish a representative Indigenous body to advise Parliament on laws and policies affecting Indigenous peoples". Similar results were reflected in other national polls including YouGov and Essential.

Crucially, there was strong support across the political spectrum for the Voice. Even a majority of Liberal National Party voters supported the establishment of the Voice, and only One Nation voters were strongly against it. But once the campaign got underway, this public support came under attack from all sides.

In September 2022, the federal Greens spokesperson on First Nations, Senator Lidia Thorpe, began attacking the Voice publicly, calling it "a waste of money".

In November 2022, the National Party said it would be campaigning for a "No" vote despite that fact that the Referendum question had not even been announced at that stage. They were soon followed in April 2023 by the Liberal Party. Their campaign, based on spreading doubt and confusion ("If you don't know, vote No"), was effective in switching the vote of those who were well-intentioned but vulnerable to a message based on fear of what the Voice supposedly might mean.

Meanwhile, far-right groups such as Advance Australia, funded by mining billionaires and advised by US firms expert in Trump-era misinformation and disinformation, spread openly racist messages. As a result, the polls that had been initially so positive swung against the "Yes" campaign, so that on the day of the poll we were left hoping for a miracle.

Our time visiting the polling booths in outer Brisbane was not hopeful. In fact, it was downright distressing. Despite the wonderful work of our volunteers and the kind support of many voters, among many the mood was resentful. Many voters avoided eye contact with us, refused to acknowledge us when we spoke to them, even knocking our hands away when we offered them a flyer outlining the reasons to support the Voice.

By the time we got back to the offices late in the afternoon and began waiting for the results to come in, we were expecting the worst.

And we got it. It was all over too soon. Three-quarters of an hour after the polls closed, it was clear we — and, in my view, the nation — had lost.

One of our friends and supporters there, a normally very mild-mannered and thoughtful person, expressed what we were all feeling: "They couldn't even give us one bloody hour."

Just as in the voting lines at the booths, we had held our hands out in friendship and in the spirit of reconciliation, and our hands had been knocked aside.

After the defeat of the Referendum, we declared a week of silence to grieve the result. The attention of the media and commentators and politicians moved on quickly. That, I suppose, is the nature of the world we live in now. But for me, and for many First Nations people, it couldn't be like that. This was another blow to bear, just the most recent of many in our history. But it could not be the final one.

It has taken a long period of reflection and conversation to make sense of the result and to start to think about what the next steps might be for us, Australia's First Peoples. What is clear is that we are now at a fork in the road. We can either continue down the path of reconciliation, to make further attempts to repair the relationship between our ancient cultures and those who have come here in the last few hundred years. We can continue — as we have always done — to fight for rights and concessions from a colonial system that seems reluctant to acknowledge us at best and downright hostile to us at worst.

Or we can take another path and conclude — as Marcia Langton did on the night of the Referendum and in her essay[1] — that "reconciliation is dead". If we take this path, we focus not on our relationship with the colonisers, but on strengthening our own families, communities and organisations, on putting into practice our right to self-determination.

Let me unpack what these two paths look like.

The first path means that we continue the long history of doing the heavy lifting in this relationship between black and white Australia. Because it has always been *us* who have tried to explain, cajole, inform and persuade those in power to recognise our rights to health, land, equality and justice, and to put in place the structures we need to enjoy those basic rights.

The Uluru Statement from the Heart is the latest in a long history that includes the 1934 petition from the Australian Aborigines' League to the English King George V asking for Aboriginal representation in federal Parliament (the Australian Government refused to send the petition to the King).

It includes the series of bark petitions from the Yolngu people of Arnhem Land, from the 1960s onwards, and the Barunga Statement presented to Prime Minister Bob Hawke in 1988 and calling for self-determination, a national system of land rights, compensation, an end to discrimination, respect for Aboriginal identity, and the granting of social, economic and cultural rights. The Barunga Statement remains imprisoned under glass at Parliament House in Canberra while its demands remain unmet.

Each time, we have tried with all the sophistication and imagination and creativity and philosophy of our diverse ancient cultures to find the right words, the words that will cut through, the words that will unlock the door to the colonial prison in which we have been placed. With each of these, we may have won minor concessions, but the cell door remains locked.

And if we continue down this path, we have to ask ourselves how are we to make progress on the other demands of the Uluru Statement — Makarrata (truthtelling) and Treaty?

The convention at Uluru made it clear that the Voice needed to come first, because we need a national body of our people with the authority given to them by our grassroots communities to progress these other matters. In the absence of the Voice, who will oversee a process of Makarrata? Who will negotiate the Treaty? And, in light of the Referendum's defeat, what chance is there of a genuine treaty being agreed?

If we take the second path, we instead focus on rebuilding a sense of grassroots collective action and optimism among our peoples. I think here about the defeat of our attempt to get a national framework for land rights agreed with government in the mid-1980s, after two decades of campaigning. After that defeat, many of our activists and leaders went home to their lands and their communities and put their efforts into local campaigns and growing up their community-controlled organisations: land councils, health services, legal services and others. This proved to be a wise and powerful response, as those organisations then nurtured and led the next generation of activism in our communities.

We can react to the defeat by going back to the local level to build a foundation of self-belief and a renewed assurance that we can change the world from the bottom up.

I remind myself that despite the incredible pressures people are under the ideals of self-reliance and self-determination have never disappeared among our mob and remain as strong as ever. I see it at a local community meeting, and there in the back of the room is a small group of older Aboriginal women, not saying much but exerting a quiet authority — and I know these women are watching over and encouraging and guarding the success of an early childhood program for the community or some such.

I see it on a small piece of Aboriginal land in remote northern Australia where a family has set up a training camp to get young people into work, complete with hot showers, a laundry, good food and a billy bubbling away — once again people are exercising their authority and their determination to make a better world not just for themselves but for their family and for the next generation.

I look at our network of Aboriginal organisations and see the same spirit there: a collective, community spirit and a practical optimism about changing the world.

The second path is all about sponsoring, facilitating, linking up and spreading such examples of our confidence, capability and pride. Setting up our own schools, health services, universities and running them our way. Perhaps this path holds the key to transforming the hurt and the anger at the Referendum result into something positive, something beautiful. But I also acknowledge that we will have to put effort into our relationship with the nation state.

The fact is that we will continue to walk both paths, as we have been compelled to do since 1788: seeking to strengthen and empower our own people, while trying to win rights from the non-Aboriginal system. The question is where the emphasis lies.

Since 2010 when Prime Minister Julia Gillard established an Expert Panel to inquire into constitutional recognition for our peoples, we have sunk enormous amounts of political, emotional and community energy into this project. How much more effort do we put into such processes? We were asked by the government: "How do you want to be recognised in the constitution?" And through the most extensive consultative exercise ever taken — the Regional Dialogues and then the Convention at Uluru in May 2017 — we gave our answer.

But to many of those in power in Australia it was the "wrong" answer: they successfully organised against it and the Referendum was defeated, despite the 6.2 million Australians who extended their hands in friendship to us by voting "Yes".

And so, where to next? It will take time for the answer to that question to emerge. A new generation of Aboriginal leaders is coming forward and each generation will make its own impact in its own way.

As a first step, we need to get back out to First Nations communities and Uluru Dialogue delegates for important conversations about what happened and where to next.

There is hurt and anger, but these emotions can be powerful motivators for action. We can move on from here with the strength and creativity that our peoples have always shown, nurtured by our relationships with each other, with our communities, and with this land.

The Referendum is only the end of another stage of our long journey. I believe it can lead us to new paths to self-determination based on our connection to our lands, communities and families, and our innate strengths of resilience and creativity.

1   Langton (2023) "Whatever the outcome, reconciliation is dead" *The Saturday Paper*

Free Her Speech: Violence Against Women and Anti-SLAPP Laws for Australia

Jennifer Robinson

Australia is in the midst of what our Prime Minister has acknowledged is a "national crisis".[1] The statistics on violence against women are shocking: one in three Australian women experience physical violence in their lifetime, while one in five experience sexual violence — with Indigenous women, women with disability and LGBTQ women experiencing violence at even higher rates.[2] What's even more shocking is that the figures are getting worse, not better. Sex Discrimination Commissioner Dr Anna Cody recently confirmed that male violence against women is *increasing*.[3] We are seeing an epidemic of violence against women. At one point in early 2024, a woman was murdered every four days.[4] But it's not just Australia, it's everywhere. UN Women has described violence against women and girls as one of the most prevalent human rights violations in the world.[5]

It's a problem that affects all of us. Whether or not we know about it, whether or not we want to acknowledge it, the statistics tell us it has happened to women we know — and it's perpetrated by men we know. And we should talk about it. My courageous grandmother, Philippa Cracknell, left my violent grandfather at a time when women only received state support if they were abandoned — not when they chose to leave violence — and she struggled to make ends meet as a single mother. She later ran refuges in Sydney for women fleeing domestic violence and helped women and children access services to rebuild their lives. I spent time with her in the refuges as a child and saw firsthand the pervasive, harmful effects of male violence, the life-saving impact of her work and how crucial well-funded frontline services are. It was a conversation with her some years ago that inspired my work on gender-based violence and free speech. She was lamenting the fact that, in the two decades since she had retired, the statistics on violence had not improved. For all the advances made towards equality in the last century — suffrage, women's ability to work, reproductive autonomy, controlling our finances — women are still vulnerable in the intimate spaces where we should feel most safe, not to mention our workplaces, schools, universities and even on the streets. My grandmother had done her bit. What was I doing about it?

Soon after in 2017, the #MeToo movement gained worldwide prominence: women were breaking cultural silence to speak about their experience of violence. The power of women speaking out en masse brought about a reckoning. Many powerful men were finally brought to account by the sheer number of accusers coming forward, encouraged by each other. In some cases, criminal convictions and professional consequences followed. The police and the criminal-justice system so often fail women — for example, only 2% of rape cases are ever successfully prosecuted — so by speaking out about their abusers, women were warning other women and holding men to account for their violence.

But what soon followed was the weaponisation of the law to

silence women and maintain the status quo — making visible the legal tools men used, from defamation claims to non-disclosure agreements. The UN Special Rapporteur on freedom of opinion and expression, Irene Khan, has since described this legal backlash as the "perverse twist" of the MeToo movement.[6] It was this legal backlash that prompted me into action — and showed me how I could continue my grandmother's work in my own way. In our book, *How Many More Women?*, Dr Keina Yoshida and I document what we were seeing in our legal practice — how the law was being weaponised globally to silence public-interest speech about gender-based violence and how this is a violation not only of freedom of expression, but of women's rights to equality and to live free from violence. Our research showed it was happening everywhere, including Australia. (The only reason I can write here about my grandfather being violent without the risk of being sued is because he died years ago — and in Australia you can't defame the dead.) If we cannot talk about male violence against women, then we cannot understand the extent of it, and we cannot even begin to address the problem.

Many have questioned whether Australia's defamation laws stifled the burgeoning #MeToo movement here, pointing to the raft of claims we have seen against women and the media — from Geoffrey Rush to Craig McLachlan to Don Burke and Christian Porter. It wasn't until 2021 that the mass March4Justice protests took place across Australia, spurred by a series of young women coming forward, including Brittany Higgins. Brittany's brave decision to speak out resulted in a raft of important reforms in Parliament and elsewhere to improve workplace safety for women. But it has also spurred no fewer than 14 defamation claims[7] — including Bruce Lehrmann's unsuccessful claim against Lisa Wilkinson and Network 10, in which he claimed Brittany lied. But in April 2024, Justice Lee found it was Lehrmann who had told "deliberate lies",[8] that his account of the night in question was "risible"[9] and "nonsense"[10] and that, on the balance of probabilities, he had raped Brittany.[11] But it took three years, Brittany being cross-examined live online about her rape in front of tens of thousands of people, and millions in legal costs, for the media to be able to defend Brittany's truth and for her to receive vindication.

How many women are going to come forward when they see what Brittany has been put through? How many in the media will report on violence against women when they see the millions in costs and scrutiny that Lisa Wilkinson and Network 10 faced?[12] The result is a deterrent for anyone else to speak out — or report on it. And that is not in the public interest.

But it's the cases we don't hear about that we should also be worried about. We simply don't have data about the number of defamation claims being threatened to silence victim-survivors and stop the media from reporting their stories. Defamation-threat letters are common, but private — and often result in self-censorship that the public does not see. Our research, and my legal practice, shows that cases like that of Brittany Higgins are merely the tip of the iceberg.

There is a way we can limit the silencing effect in Australia: anti-SLAPP legislation. SLAPPs are "strategic lawsuits against public participation" — that is, lawsuits designed to silence activists and journalists, often brought by the rich and powerful to cover up wrongdoing. The threat of a lawsuit and crippling legal costs is often enough to silence. Until recently, SLAPPs were often associated with stifling environmental activism and advocacy and silencing reporting on environmental or financial crimes. For example, at the time of the assassination of the courageous investigative journalist Daphne Caruana Galizia in Malta, there were 47 defamation suits pending against her.[13] These were all SLAPPs — lawsuits designed to silence my client's fearless public-interest reporting on political corruption. As Keina and I argue in our book, defamation claims aimed at silencing journalists and women speaking out about gender-based violence are also SLAPPs — they are limiting women's public participation, shutting down public-interest discussion about violence against women, and perpetuating abuse, giving abusers impunity.

Anti-SLAPP legislation has long existed in the US. It empowers judges to stop claims that are an abuse of the legal process, that is, where the claims seek to silence speech in the public interest. And it can protect women speaking about their experience of abuse. For example, it could have protected my client Amber Heard from the defamation claim brought against her by her ex-husband Johnny Depp in the US. We had already proven in a British court that Depp had been repeatedly violent towards her.[14] But he then sued her for defamation in Virginia — a state where neither of them lived — because, unlike in California where they lived, Virginia had no anti-SLAPP laws that would have protected her — and her speech. Amber was almost bankrupted by that US defamation claim, which she lost after a problematic and fundamentally flawed jury trial.[15] Earlier this year, those same anti-SLAPP provisions in California were used to dismiss Marilyn Manson's defamation suit against his ex-partner, Evan Rachel Wood, who had alleged he was sexually violent.[16] In 2024, the European Parliament introduced anti-SLAPP legislation ("Daphne's law") in honour of Daphne Caruana Galizia. The UK is debating similar laws.

In Australia this isn't even a conversation — and it needs to be. The ACT is the only jurisdiction with laws resembling anti-SLAPP protections, but defamation claims are not covered.[17] As a country that now beats London as the libel capital of the world — and with so many claims being filed in relation to women's speech about alleged violence — it is vital that lawmakers consider anti-SLAPP legislation to deter litigation which stifles public-interest discussion about gender-based violence. We cannot begin to deal with or end violence against women if we can't talk about it or report on it.

Jennifer Robinson would like to thank Dr Keina Yoshida and Phoebe Cook for their contributions to this piece.

1. Massola and Chrysanthos (2024), https://www.smh.com.au/politics/federal/albanese-admits-domestic-violence-is-national-crisis-20240428-p5fn2d.html
2. Our Watch Institute, https://www.ourwatch.org.au/quick-facts
3. Cody (2024) "The Truth About the Men Who Kill Women" https://7ampodcast.com.au/episodes/the-truth-about-men-who-kill-women
4. Lyons (2024), https://www.theguardian.com/australia-news/article/2024/may/05/horror-and-fury-in-australia-as-epidemic-of-violence-against-women-sweeps-across-the-country
5. UN Women, https://www.unwomen.org/en/what-we-do/ending-violence-against-women/faqs/types-of-violence
6. Special Rapporteur on the promotion and protection of the right to freedom of opinion and expression, "Gender justice and freedom of expression", (2021), A/76/258, para 22
7. Robinson and Yoshida (2024) *How Many More Women*, Allen & Unwin, p 422
8. *Lehrmann v Network Ten Pty Limited Trial Judgment* (2024) FCA 369, 153
9. *Lehrmann v Network Ten Pty Limited Trial Judgment* (2024) FCA 369, 421
10. *Lehrmann v Network Ten Pty Limited Trial Judgment* (2024) FCA 369, 131
11. *Lehrmann v Network Ten Pty Limited Trial Judgment* (2024) FCA 369, 620-621
12. Robinson (2022) "After watching how Brittany Higgins has suffered, how many women will be silenced?" https://www.theguardian.com/commentisfree/2022/dec/06/after-watching-how-brittany-higgins-has-suffered-how-many-women-will-be-silenced?trk=public_post_feed-article-content
13. Robinson and Yoshida p 373
14. Robinson and Yoshida pp 315–326
15. Robinson and Yoshida pp 326–340
16. Robinson and Yoshida p 409
17. Robinson and Yoshida p 410

Action for Green Transformation Needs Politics of Inclusion

Sunita Narain

People across the world stand at crossroads — the challenge of unsustainable growth means that we are hurtling towards climate catastrophe and the challenge of inequitable growth means that we are hurtling towards increased poverty, increased marginalisation and increased anger. What we have learned in India is that unaffordable growth, in other words inequitable growth, cannot be sustainable. This is the agenda for the future.

My city, Delhi, has become infamous for its toxic pollution. But it is not that we are not trying to make a difference. There is outrage in the city because of pollution; there is action. All coal plants have been shut; pet coke, which the US exports because it is too toxic for local use, has been banned; and we are moving to the cleanest fuels and vehicle technology. So, we are acting. But it is not good enough. Every winter, pollution is back with a vengeance. My colleagues have estimated that air pollution in Delhi is down by 25% over the past three years, as compared to the previous three years; but we still need to decrease by 65% to get what we call clean air.

And this is when air pollution is a great equaliser. It does not differentiate between the rich and the poor; between the rural and urban. This is different from water pollution, since the rich can move to drinking bottled water. And so, even if our rivers are polluted, clean water is affordable for the relatively rich. However, when it comes to air pollution, it is different. The airshed of the city is the same for the rich and the poor. The middle and upper classes can buy air purifiers but still have to breathe — and this airshed includes the toxins from the cars of the rich and the biomass-based stoves of the poor.

This is where the question of what we do next becomes critical. We can continue to do what the rest of the world has done to combat pollution from each vehicle. We can also improve the quality of fuel and even consider moving to electric vehicles. But these incremental actions keep us spending and keep us behind the pollution crisis.

The reason is simple: today less than 20% of people in my city drive in cars to work; roughly 25% own cars. But these vehicle owners take 90% of the road space. The question is: if the demand of just 20% is leading to huge congestion and pollution, where and how can the city find the road and air space for all?

This is where the environmentalism of the poor will kick in. The fact is that if the rich are to breathe clean air, we need to rework mobility for all. We cannot think of adding a few buses or trams or metros; we need to transform mobility so that it works for the rich and the poor. This will mean combining affordability *and* convenience *and* safety.

This is also the case with energy. Today, many households in my country still use biomass to cook their food. Women are exposed to toxic air pollutants. But they do this because they are poor. The problem is that this pollution, which is also killing poor people, is contaminating the same airshed — the airshed of the rich. If we want clean air, we have to get the rich out of their polluting vehicles, but we will also have to ensure that the poor women get options to move away from dirty fuels. Their energy transition is important for clean air. Without inclusive growth, we cannot have sustainability.

The opportunity is also enormous. If we reinvent for transformative action we will focus on the needs of the poor women and provide them viable, affordable options to leapfrog — to go from dirty non-fossil fuels, not to fossil fuels, but to clean energy. This is where nations need to collaborate and for this we need leadership so that finance for the energy transition is concessional and provides the opportunity to scale up the system for the poorest in the world.

The challenge of climate change is a mirror to the air pollution challenge we face in Delhi. In 1990, my colleague Anil Agarwal and I argued in our publication *Global Warming in an Unequal World* that the world cannot combat climate change unless the agreement is fair and equitable. Today, the same issue is on the table. If the solutions cannot meet the needs of all — if they are not equitable — it will not work. We need to understand the environmentalism of the poor.

It is clear events in our world are now spiralling out of control. Every year we are told is the hottest year, till the next year comes around. Then a new record is broken. It is getting worse. From forest fires, to increasing frequency and intensity of storms, to blistering cold fronts and scorching heat.

Let's also be clear that we have a most inconvenient truth. At current rates, the world will run out of the carbon budget — how much it can emit to keep below 1.5°C — by 2030. But there are vast numbers of people who do not have access to basic energy. They still need to grow; they need energy for their development.

It is also clear that increasing numbers of disasters because of growing intensity and frequency of extreme weather will make the poor, poorer. Their impoverishment and marginalisation will add to their desperation to move away from their lands and to seek alternative livelihoods. Their only choice will be to migrate — move to the city; move to another country. The double-jeopardy, as I have called it, in the interconnected world is the push, or lack of option, to the pull, bright lights that suggest a choice of better futures. This will add to the already volatile situation of boat people and walls and migrant counting, which is making our world insecure and violent. This is the cycle of destructive change that we must fight. Our globalised world is interconnected and interdependent. It is something we must recognise.

Sustainable development is not possible if it is not equitable. Growth must be affordable and inclusive for it to be sustainable. But all this will not happen unless we articulate that the environmental challenge is not technocratic but political. We cannot neuter politics of access, justice and rights and hope to fix the environment or indeed development. This is why we need cooperation so that future development can be low carbon for all.

Culture, Money and Morals

Louise Adler AM

It is now incontrovertible that an Australian culture exists, is appreciated and supported by the citizenry and has international resonance. That's the good news. The bad? Government funding for the arts has declined in real terms over the past four decades; audiences are voting with their wallets and have declared their preference for Netflix over live performing arts.

In the ever-widening gap between government funding and prohibitive ticket prices certain outcomes are inevitable. The corporatisation of arts boards has often paradoxically resulted in amateurish governance, increasing reliance on philanthropy and sponsorship and a concomitant escalation in influence over artistic decisions. The relationship between boards, management and artists is fragile and becoming increasingly fraught.

A catalogue of woes has built over a decade or two. Locally and internationally, a succession of arts organisations across all sectors has come under pressure from artists (surely their first and most important stakeholders) to "take a stand" on a range of topical issues from the climate crisis to Israel's war on Gaza.

There is nothing new about artists being engaged with the issues of the day. In 1937 British writers were asked to declare whether they were for or against Franco and fascism: "it is impossible any longer to take no side" and an anthology was published — *Authors Take Sides*. The anthology emerged again during the Falklands, Vietnam, and Iraq and Gulf wars.

When MUP decided to publish an Australian edition, I asked Frank Moorhouse to contribute. His rhetorical retort was to ask why I wasn't proposing a collection titled *Dentists Take Sides*. Nonetheless he delivered his own robust contribution. But the question persists: should we expect artists and their work to engage with the issues of the day? And if we do, what is the appropriate response of the boards and managers of arts organisations? A degree of misalignment is unavoidable.

Many artists feel a moral obligation to use their voices and their art to speak to the injustices and cruelties of the times. Would we wish artists to be indifferent, to narcissistically ignore the world in which they make their art? Even the 19th century artist in his (most often male) garret could not be immune to the life outside his door.

Last year three actors in Sydney took a curtain call wearing keffiyeh. The usual cultural sentries hyperventilated, ratcheting outrage across column acres. On opening night, well-heeled titans of commerce and finance became suddenly fearful in their premium seats, feeling unsafe and intimidated by impecunious artists with different opinions.

These captains of industry withdrew their financial support and closed their chequebooks. Emails circulated encouraging donors across the nation to join them and withdraw funding from those arts organisations which had responded to artists' demands for statements calling for a ceasefire and an end to the occupation.

There is a long tradition in the Jewish community of generous support for the arts. In the Muslim community, giving 10% of one's wealth to charitable causes is a moral imperative. Historically, donors tended to prefer the anonymity of genuine philanthropy free from self-aggrandisement. What has changed is the sense of entitlement: donations now come with expectations, seats at the board table and judgements about curatorial decisions. A further evolution this century has seen second and third generations keen to have "relationships" with the organisations they choose to support: naming of buildings and programs, expectations of invitations, of being feted, wined and dined and of the omnipresent complimentary tickets.

When accepting the corporate or donor dime it is probably worth remembering the aphorism that one needs a long spoon to sup with the devil. Who can forget *Curb Your Enthusiasm*'s take on philanthropy? On hearing that his rival Ted Danson is donating to a worthy cause, Larry David matches him. At the opening party to laud donors, Larry is horrified to discover that he's been outdone, Ted's donation being listed as "anonymous". Everyone "knows" who this is but deems it the more modest gesture. Anonymity is seen as genuine altruism, while Larry's is a grandstanding gesture.

This year Baillie Gifford, one of the largest corporate sponsors of the arts (and in particular of literary culture) in the UK withdrew its support from literary festivals after a Fossil Free Books (FFB) campaign linked its protest to the climate crisis and Israel's war on Gaza. Some festival organisers felt "bullied" by the artist–activists' threat of a boycott of their events and were encouraged by some literary luminaries with opposing views to resist the pressure. Hay Festival is now short £130,000, Edinburgh International Book Festival is down £350,000. At least ten UK literary festivals are now imperilled as a consequence. This means fewer opportunities for writers to discuss their work, promote their books and publicise their concerns before huge and attentive crowds.

Had the FFB campaign been such a smart strategy? One writer asked pointedly why activists had not focused on the "real enemies" — calling on colleagues to "withdraw their labour" and strike against the Murdocracy for example, by refusing to publish with HarperCollins, or demanding to be deleted from *The Times* bestseller lists. Another argued that among all corrupt and complicit corporations, Baillie Gifford is a mere minnow.

Those of us now working in arts organisations share gallows humour while spending endless executive hours drafting risk analyses to assuage nervous boards. The reality is that risk is inevitable, buffeted by mass-media opinionistas and social-media warriors. Meanwhile, artists require board directors with fortitude and a commitment to support the artistic vision. There needs to be a shared recognition that art is by its very nature unpredictable, all arts consumers can never be satisfied, and no box-office revenues guaranteed.

So, what might good cultural leadership look like? Fundamentally, the tail should not wag the dog — those tails include the government of the day, donors and sponsors. If boards resent the pressure they feel from artists, I think they forget that organisations exist to enable artists and their work.

When Adelaide Writers' Week in 2023 showcased Palestinian contemporary writing there was a media flurry engendered by antagonists. I remember the leadership shown by the former chair of Adelaide Festival who robustly responded to the withdrawal of one corporate sponsor by asserting they weren't the sort of sponsor we wanted.

Arts organisations require directors with legal, financial and political expertise. But directors must understand the core business of the organisations. Artists need to be appointed to arts boards and to be taken seriously. Boards need an appetite for risk, clarity in the mandate and confidence in both the artform and the audience.

Finally, government relationships must be at arm's length, holding fast to the principle of curatorial independence. The long-term sustainability of arts organisations is under threat, once again, from a lack of funding, poor governance, declining and ageing audiences and a lack of courageous leadership.

Destination Disaster: The Urgent Call from the Pacific Island People

His Excellency Anote Tong

In an era marked by technological progress and geopolitical tensions unseen since World War II, humanity finds itself at a critical juncture. The very innovations intended to alleviate global hardships have exacerbated existential threats to our planet. As I reflect from my village, connected yet distant from the centres of power, I witness a world grappling with the Russia/Ukraine conflict, Middle Eastern tensions, and escalating disputes in the Asia-Pacific region, alongside sobering scientific updates on climate change.

Climate change, in particular, stands as the paramount moral challenge of our time. Despite overwhelming scientific consensus and calls for action by organisations like the United Nations and its various bodies, including the Intergovernmental Panel on Climate Change (IPCC), the international community remains mired in indecision. Throughout my presidency, I have consistently stressed Kiribati's vulnerability to climate change. Representations to successive Australian administrations and currently an ongoing Parliamentary Committee underscore our region's unwavering stance on climate change as the greatest security threat, emphasising the urgent need for effective global action.

Yet, collective global political will remains stymied by narrower national economic interests, including in countries like Australia and New Zealand, where climate action is often sidelined in favour of economic growth. This short-sighted approach ignores the devastating impacts already felt in places like the Marshall Islands, Tuvalu and Kiribati, where rising seas have begun to imperil homes and livelihoods. This political challenge has been a consistent theme in my advocacy, where I've highlighted the need for sustained and principled global action, transcending national interests to address the universal threat of climate change.

The concept of "regulatory capture", where industry interests subvert regulatory intent, looms large in discussions of governance failures. The stark reality is that while scientific understanding grows sharper, political responses remain inadequate and are often compromised. This phenomenon compromises effective responses to climate change, undermining efforts to enact meaningful change. Throughout my presidency, I have highlighted the detrimental impact of regulatory capture on climate policy, highlighting the need for transparent and accountable governance frameworks that prioritise environmental stewardship over corporate profits.

Looking ahead, the United Nations, despite its noble intentions, has yet to provide the decisive action needed to avert disaster. IPCC reports, from Assessment Report IV in 2007 to the latest Assessment Report VI in 2021, provide increasingly dire projections. They warn that even with immediate cessation of greenhouse-gas emissions, inertia in the climate system will render many low-lying island nations uninhabitable by 2060. This stark reality necessitates a shift from just focusing on emissions reduction to comprehensive support for communities facing irreversible impacts. This urgency has been a central theme in my advocacy, where I've consistently called for global solidarity and immediate action to address the existential threat faced by vulnerable communities like Kiribati.

In advocating for our survival, I have consistently called for "migration with dignity" as a humane response to the inevitable displacement of our people. Relocation plans must prioritise preserving cultural identity and community cohesion, mitigating the trauma of displacement. This approach has been a cornerstone of my presidency and continues to guide our efforts to secure a sustainable future for Kiribati and other vulnerable Pacific island nations.

As we navigate these moral quandaries, it is evident that our collective humanity is being tested. The choices we make today will define the future not just for our generation but for all who inherit this planet. This sentiment has been echoed in my past speeches and writings, emphasising the moral imperative of global solidarity in addressing climate change. I have consistently urged world leaders to transcend narrow national interests and embrace a shared responsibility for environmental stewardship, highlighting the interconnectedness of global climate impacts and the urgent need for collaborative action.

Despite scientific consensus and international agreements like the Paris Agreement, progress in addressing climate change remains painfully slow and inadequate. The commitments made by global powers often fall short of what is required to keep global temperature rise below catastrophic levels. This gap between rhetoric and action perpetuates the suffering of vulnerable communities like those in Kiribati, who bear the brunt of climate change despite contributing minimally to global emissions.

The concept of "climate justice" has gained traction in recent years, highlighting the moral imperative of addressing climate change through an equitable process. It demands that those least responsible for climate change but most affected by its impacts receive support and solidarity from the international community. This principle has guided my advocacy efforts, underscoring the need for developed nations to fulfill their obligations to vulnerable countries through financial assistance, technology transfer, and capacity-building initiatives.

In the face of these challenges, adaptation strategies are crucial for communities like Kiribati to build resilience against the impacts of climate change. This includes infrastructure improvements, early-warning systems for extreme weather events, and sustainable resource management practices. However, adaptation alone is insufficient without concurrent efforts to mitigate greenhouse-gas emissions and curb the drivers of climate change.

The role of education and awareness cannot be overstated in fostering a global understanding of climate change and its impacts. In Kiribati, we have prioritised environmental education to empower our youth with the knowledge and skills to become stewards of our natural resources. This investment in education is not just about preparing future generations to confront climate challenges but also about instilling a sense of responsibility and agency in shaping a sustainable future.

In conclusion, the fate of our planet hinges on our ability to transcend narrow national interests and embrace global solidarity in the face of climate change. The crisis demands a re-evaluation of governance structures and economic paradigms that prioritise profit over sustainability. Only through concerted international cooperation and bold action can we safeguard the future of vulnerable communities and preserve the planet for generations to come.

The lessons learned from Kiribati's experience show the urgency of climate action and the moral imperative of protecting our planet's most vulnerable populations. As we confront the challenges ahead, let us heed the warnings of science and the calls of conscience to forge a path towards a sustainable and equitable future for all.

First Nations Powering the Energy Transition

Karrina Nolan

As the world enters a new phase of protecting, managing and developing our land and sea, our people must be central to the transition towards clean energy. Our aspirations for protecting communities' rights and interests and building economic self-determination with the renewables revolution can be powered by us, on our Country and in our homes, on our terms.

We are aware of the scale of the transition and the task before us — the largest shift in how energy is generated, moved, stored and used in our lifetime. In Australia over the next few decades, we are going to see an enormous amount of renewables and energy infrastructure built on our Country, if we consent.

We need to remind ourselves that the driver for the transition is climate change and the critical need to keep the planet below 1.5°C warming. Indigenous peoples the world over continue to be the stewards and custodians of biodiversity of sacred places of our cultural heritage. Our brothers and sisters from the Torres Strait and communities right across the nation are threatened by rising seas, floods and fires. People are increasingly unable to stay on homelands or in town camps because regions where we are living have some of the highest temperatures on the planet, and there is no way to keep some of our homes adequately cool or warm due to substandard housing, outdated energy infrastructure and expensive and irregular power supplies.

Despite the challenges, however, many of these same communities have developed solutions backed up by the sheer determination to innovate, work together and solve problems.

One thing we are clear about is that we can't simply swap one kind of energy for another without transforming the systems that go with them. We need to bring a different mindset or we run the risk of repeating the mistakes of the past. Australia has a history of land theft and resource extraction at any cost. This has had a major impact on our land and waters, our families and communities. And while there is absolutely an urgency to scale up clean energy, we need to ensure the transition is done the right way, with justice. Without our people, this transition cannot be done.

In the last few years through being organised across the country and as a national First Nations Clean Energy Network[1], we have grown our power, changed the story on what is expected from industry and are increasingly included in the government's plans for a clean energy rollout.

What does it look like when the energy transition is powered by us? When our ideas are backed and resourced, when our leadership is listened to, when our knowledge genuinely shapes projects and our consent informs the direction of economic development?

For the transition to be done well, in addition to genuine engagement and consent, our people need access to clean, affordable and reliable power. When our people are disconnected from power, food goes off, medicines can't be kept cool, and heating and cooling is a serious issue, with many households using air conditioning in just one room over summer for people to take turns sleeping in.

Residential rooftop solar is now the cheapest energy in the world, and for over 3.5 million Australian households, disconnections and expensive energy bills belong to the past. This is absolutely *not* the case for the majority of our people. Subsidies have *not* been accessible for batteries and panels. Transport and installation costs are high. Regulations are difficult to navigate. Removing regulatory and financing barriers will enable our people to install rooftop solar on our homes and in our communities.

For those living in rental, social or public housing, additional policy reform is needed, including certainty around responsibility for procurement, ownership and maintenance of renewable and energy-efficient assets in the home.

And in the commercial sphere, as we develop more export projects on Country, we must in turn consider the energy needs of those who need it most. The Canadians are doing amazing work on this front. There, First Nations peoples are partners or beneficiaries of almost 20% of renewable energy initiatives[2], and the majority (52%) of at least 135 major energy and related projects[3] have some form of Indigenous ownership.[4] Its government-funded program moving communities off diesel[5] combined with upgrading social housing stock to a better energy rating is one such example.

The Canadian Government recognised some time ago that investing in Indigenous-led, clean-energy projects[6] based on local priorities[7] and innovative solutions reduces risk and project costs and increases economic participation and reconciliation.

Canada's 2023 Budget dedicated $60 billion to clean-energy tax credits and $20 billion to sustainable infrastructure investments with $3 billion slated for various regional priorities and Indigenous-led projects. Its 2024 Budget proposed a $5 billion Indigenous Loan Guarantee program[8], which represents a significant opportunity to foster economic growth and energy sovereignty in Indigenous and

First Nations communities where local people make the decisions based on local priorities.

In the United States, the Inflation Reduction Act (IRA) of 2023 similarly recognised that First Nations have always played a role as stewards, and now have a role to play in the energy transition. The IRA introduced significant shifts to the Tribal Nations' energy development landscape through rebates, loans, guarantees and tax credits, also setting aside $720 million in grants incentivising Tribal Nations' building of clean energy projects in communities that used to host fossil fuel infrastructure.

The Australian government's announcement on 25 June 2024[9] that First Nations' benefits and principles will be incorporated into the *Future Made in Australia Act*[10] will finally bring Australia onto a more equal footing with the United States and Canada.

This follows two previous positive initiatives. The new Net Zero Economy Authority Bill 2024[11] establishing the Net Zero Economy Authority mandates supporting First Nations persons "to participate in, and benefit from, Australia's transition to a net zero emissions economy". And the *National Reconstruction Fund Corporation Act 2023*[12] mandates the Board recognise "the desirability of encouraging and improving economic participation by historically underrepresented groups, including ... First Nations Australians".

These two existing examples stand as powerful precedent for ensuring First Nations participation and benefit is specifically included in the *Future Made in Australia Act*. Yet, while this big policy and investment focus is necessary to change the energy landscape and ensure First Nations people can build a First Nations economy, government and industry remain slow to invest in small-scale housing and community initiatives.

The Australian Energy Market Operator projects some 90 gigawatts of solar (from near 20 gigawatts currently) will be needed on rooftops (with a mixture of other distributed solar resources) among other measures by 2050. This requires policy settings and resourcing in place to support the pace and equitable distribution beyond the National Electricity Market's eastern seaboard and renewable energy zones.

There are around 300,000 First Nations homes in Australia with limited access to reliable and affordable clean power. Let us reform policy and power these homes with renewables, switch out diesel generators, increase the energy efficiency of households, build in climate-resilient retrofits, and build a local workforce at the same time. Our communities are working on these and more local solutions.

As we live with more extreme weather conditions, a secure climate-resilient power supply and long-life local storage systems are critical to keep the power on, reduce electricity costs, create local jobs, and build economic empowerment. Experience tells us to start small and grow and resource the capacity and ability of our Traditional Owners to shape local solutions and make local decisions.

We all know this transition presents extraordinary challenges but also incredible opportunities. We need to back and resource the leadership of our communities and the custodians who are the first and oldest line of protection of sacred places and lands and waters upon which we all depend.

1   First Nations Clean Energy Network (n.d.) *Join us in driving Australia's clean energy revolution!*, https://www.firstnationscleanenergy.org.au/
2   Gall et al (2022) *Waves of Change*, https://climateinstitute.ca/wp-content/uploads/2022/02/ICE-report-ENGLISH-FINAL.pdf
3   Worland (2024) "Want More Clean Energy Projects? Give Communities a Stake", *TIME*, https://time.com/6992183/clean-energy-canada-community-ownership/
4   Carruthers and McKlusky (2024) *Update on Trends in Indigenous Equity Investments in Canada*, https://www.fasken.com/en/knowledge/2023/11/

indigenous-equity-in-energy-and-infrastructure-projects-in-canada

5   Government of Canada (2023) *Indigenous Off-Diesel Initiative*, https://www.canada.ca/en/services/environment/weather/climatechange/climate-plan/reduce-emissions/reducing-reliance-diesel/indigenous-off-diesel-initiative.html

6   Government of Canada (2024) *Wah-ila-toos: Clean Energy Initiatives in Indigenous, rural and remote communities*, https://www.canada.ca/en/services/environment/weather/climatechange/climate-plan/reduce-emissions/reducing-reliance-diesel.html

7   Government of Canada (2023) *New Indigenous Council to Play Key Role in Advancing Clean Energy Projects in Indigenous, Rural and Remote Communities*, https://www.canada.ca/en/natural-resources-canada/news/2023/02/new-indigenous-council-to-play-key-role-in-advancing-clean-energy-projects-in-indigenous-rural-and-remote-communities.html

8   Canada Development Investment Corporation (2024) *Indigenous Loan Guarantee Program*, https://cdev.gc.ca/indigenous-loan-guarantee-program/

9   First Nations Clean Energy Network (2024) *First Nations benefit to be written into Future Made in Australia Act: Minister Chris Bowen MP*, https://www.firstnationscleanenergy.org.au/first_nations_benefit

10   Kneebone (2024) "Is Australia finally catching up on clean energy benefits for First Nations?", *Renew Economy*, https://reneweconomy.com.au/is-australia-finally-catching-up-on-clean-energy-benefits-for-first-nations/

11   Net Zero Economy Authority Bill 2024, https://parlinfo.aph.gov.au/parlInfo/download/legislation/bills/r7177_third-reps/toc_pdf/24043b01.pdf;fileType=application%2Fpdf

12   *National Reconstruction Fund Corporation Act 2023* (Cth), https://www.legislation.gov.au/C2023A00012/latest/text

The Democratisation of Data for Improving Child and Family Health and Wellbeing

Professor Fiona Stanley AC and Associate Professor Rebecca Glauert

It is an honour to acknowledge and celebrate 30 years of The Australia Institute. Their aims and ours are the same: to access and use the best data to improve social, health and wellbeing policies for 21st century Australia. And, as the inscription from 1926 on the Shenton Park Child Health Centre in Western Australia reads, "the health of mother and child is the most important investment for the state". If we can optimise early healthy pathways, Australia's future human capital will be enhanced.

It is now more than 30 years since we had a dream of an institute for child health and wellbeing in WA, one that would build on the excellent population data in WA (statutory collections and total population registers) and work collaboratively with government and basic and clinical sciences to investigate the causes of the many complex issues facing children, with a major focus on prevention.

The last century produced dramatic improvements in child health.[1] From the 1970s there were increases in a range of problems called "the new morbidity" — suicide rates in males aged 15 to 19 rose fourfold between 1970 and 1990, and doubled for females. Developmental disabilities and mental health problems increased. Were these real increases or were we just recognising and diagnosing more? Child maltreatment cases increased in all states and territories[2], allergies and obesity[3] increased. The gap between Aboriginal and non-Aboriginal kids had been there since colonisation, but our data only really described the extent of this disparity from the mid-1980s when we could identify ethnicity on birth and death data.[4] These new morbidities and disparities among marginalised populations has exploded in our wealthy societies. Not just Australia but particularly in English-speaking colonised countries (such as Canada).[5]

In response to these increases in poor outcomes, and building on the existing total population data sets, as researchers, we expanded our record linkage capacity from mostly health outcomes to all aspects of child development. We recognised the importance of having "the complete picture". The social determinants of health and wellbeing are ever-present. If we only focus on one part of the picture (health), that is all we can address.

Children live outside the silos of government agencies and we couldn't continue in attempts to address these complex issues without the appropriate data to support our mission. We negotiated with relevant government agencies to link education, disability, child protection, public housing, police and justice contacts back into birth and health records. This Developmental Pathways Project (DPP) was funded by an ARC Linkage grant, engaged all the Directors General in the prioritisation of research, and rivalled similar data sets in Manitoba, Canada. Few other countries had such linked data which enabled us to follow all children from conception through school, out-of-home care, with disabilities and without, and into contacts with public housing, police and justice agencies. The strength of this model was not only that we had an ongoing cohort of the total population of WA births linked to the range of health, social and other outcomes, but that we had such close collaborations with the influential leaders in the relevant government departments.

There were two major approaches — to measure trends and their antecedents, (both causative and preventive) and to evaluate outcomes for families, which services worked, and which didn't and for whom. And we questioned whether joined-up data could influence joined-up thinking, as it became obvious that pathways into all agency contacts had common antecedents.[6] If you effectively intervene early, then outcomes in health, education, child maltreatment and detention will all improve. This was powerful and exciting evidence! Getting it right early for health improved all the major problems we were observing in our society.

And while it was clear that most of the damaging pathways commenced in poverty (especially for First Nations people), the interventions by governments were doing little to reduce this. Most services focus on the ends of pathways when interventions are ineffective and costly. This Developmental Pathways Project influenced all the social research we did in the Institute; it also enhanced many of our surveys, case-control, cohort studies and randomised controlled trials as we sought permission to link these into the DPP to enhance representation and follow-up. The data also fuelled our effective advocacy for early intervention, Aboriginal policies, prevention of birth defects, and improvements in maternal and child health, developmental services, child protection and more. It enabled us to achieve mandatory fortification of flour with folate to prevent spina bifida and related defects.

From 2015, with departmental restructures and changes in

priorities, it became harder to link and analyse the DPP (the power of these data was that we linked all records without consent, anonymously, to ensure that our analyses were not biased).[7] And sadly, privacy fears prevented us from linking federal health data, like the Pharmaceutical Benefits Scheme, to all linked health outcomes to rapidly identify the next thalidomide or adverse drug effects. We endured nearly a decade of limited capacity to analyse up-to-date linked data on the social determinants of health and wellbeing.

While developing the DPP and supporting PhD students to conduct important research into the complex issues facing Australia's children and young people, we also encountered like-minded individuals from across sectors who needed access to good data on children and young people but couldn't get it. The timelines to access data were protracted, and costs prohibitive. All of this meant that those who needed access to this information to make evidence-based decisions were simply unable to. They were forced to make, at best, guesses from anecdotal evidence, and at worst, decisions based on information they found online. This got us thinking about the democratisation of data.

If data are collected on our children and young people that have the power to improve their outcomes, then surely there is a moral and ethical obligation to make those data available for research and decision-making.

In 2023 we launched the Australian Child and Youth Wellbeing Atlas (ACYWA[8]). This atlas geographically maps data on children and young people across Australia on all health and wellbeing domains. We source data from custodians, process it, and map it. The power of this atlas is that it is freely available, and it enables the monitoring, analysis and visualisation of health and wellbeing metrics. It shines a light on the issues facing our next generation. It supports transparency and accountability. If the data are there, in the public domain, the facts cannot be denied. It enables communities to advocate for themselves. For the first time they have access to data that will help them tell their stories; it will help them get the resources they need for their communities. It puts the power back into the hands of the people and those who need it. It leads to a better, more equitable Australia.

It is deeply concerning to us that we are having the same conversation now that we were having more than 20 years ago. Despite these conversations, we are *still* seeing increases in mental health problems, we have been unable to Close the Gap, there are falling rates of good educational outcomes[9], we are facing a juvenile detention crisis and increasing numbers of children in out-of-home care.[10] Australia needs not only the best data, but we need action. While the ACYWA can help shine a light on these issues, it is imperative that we work together to rectify them: researchers; bureaucrats; clinicians; the community; and the not-for-profit sector. No one can do this alone.

It is pleasing to see progress in WA with the creation of PeopleWA, a whole-of-state linked-data asset, but we need to include Commonwealth-held data, such as Medicare, Pharmaceutical Benefits and social services data to complete the picture and truly analyse and address the impacts of inequity, policies and interventions. However, even if we do get the best data, and conduct the best research, there is little impact if it is not utilised for policy and planning.

They got it right in 1926; can we do so in 2024? We hope so, because our future generations depend on it.

1   Stanley (2001), "Child health since federation" *Millennium Yearbook Australia*; Stanley (2002), "Before the Bough Breaks, Doing More for our Children in the 21st Century" Cunningham Lecture

2   O'Donnell, Taplin, Marriott, Lima and Stanley FJ (2019) "Infant removals: The need to address the over-representation of Aboriginal infants and community concerns of another 'stolen generation'", *Child Abuse & Neglect*

3   Australian Institute of Health and Welfare (2020) "Overweight and obesity among Australian children and adolescents"

4   Seward JF and Stanley FJ (1981) "Comparison of births to Aboriginal and Caucasian mothers in Western Australia", *Medical Journal of Australia*

5   UNICEF Innocenti — Global Office of Research and Foresight, Innocenti Report Card 18 (2023): "Child poverty in the midst of wealth"

6   Stanley, Glauert, McKenzie and O'Donnell (2011)"Can joined-up data lead to joined-up thinking?" *The Western Australian developmental pathways project*

7   Stanley (2010) "Privacy or Public Good? Why not Obtaining Consent may be Best Practice", *Significance*, Vol 7, Issue 2

8   https://australianchildatlas.com

9   https://www.oecd.org/publication/pisa-2022-results/country-notes/australia-e9346d47/

10 O'Donnell, Taplin, Marriott, Lima F and Stanley FJ (2019) "Infant removals: The need to address the over-representation of Aboriginal infants and community concerns of another 'stolen generation'", *Child Abuse & Neglect* April 1990

If Australia Could Be Brave

Amy Remeikis

Think about some Australian political truisms you "know" to be true. Politics must play to the centre to have any chance of success. Change must be gradual if it's to hold. Don't shock the centre and always remember the base. Those who uphold the centre are the purveyors of sense. The feelings of the individual are paramount to those of the collective. Stick to the line and eventually they'll fall back.

Doesn't it make you tired?

Watching Australian politics is like watching a bucket of crabs — anyone who attempts to rise above the fray and promote change or a better way is pulled back into the bucket by their peers. Freedom is viewed as a finite resource; it is better for no one to have it, if it can't be you. Success is measured by how many crabs can be pulled back into the bucket, rather than how many can be freed.

Wouldn't it be wonderful if Australia could be brave?

It shouldn't seem like such a big idea. But a lack of bravery, especially in this modern era of political centrism, has seen politics drift to the right as the centre trails after to keep up with the most dominant forces, and policy stays stagnant, offending no one. Upholding the status quo.

Once-progressive politicians now find themselves so paralysed by the possibility of being dragged into a culture war, they fold at the first sign of a fight.

It has left Australia a land, politically at least, of small thinking. There is no bravery in small targets. And yet, there is a whole apparatus set up to ensure no one even thinks of thinking bigger. "Centrist" journalists will scoff at any new idea which could benefit a collective not represented by their class, lambasting left-of-centre policy offerings as "radical" or "preposterous" while never examining what their own centrist views are rooted in. Press gallery hall monitors fall over themselves to verbally whip anyone they think has transgressed without stopping to consider why they are so eager to uphold the status quo.

So, politicians and the media work to keep pulling crabs back into the bucket they dwell in, never once considering what, or whom, it is they are serving.

But imagine, for a moment, if those guiding and explaining Australia's policies were brave.

The sin of progressive or left politics is being on the right side of history too early. Of seeing the potential for a better world and trying to bring it to light before it's considered undeniably the right way. What is so radical in working towards something better? Why must Australia be tethered to those who fear, those who are so timorous of the unknown they dedicate their lives to ensuring no one steps outside of the strictures? Conservatism is forged in a certain world order, where difference is seen as a threat, rather than a thing to celebrate. The status quo will claim that its world view is protecting "freedom" and the "individual", when it's really just freedom for the few.

And for the most part, Australians fall into line. We comfort ourselves that mandatory voting and a smaller population mean we haven't fallen into the "extremes" of the United States, but we whitewash our history and rework the national narrative to suit how we like to think of ourselves.

We lack the bravery to push ahead with what is right, as we worry about the fights with those who are wrong. A brave Australia could reckon with its past and sit with Indigenous truth-telling and treaty. A brave Australia could tax land instead of labour, and make those who profit from the nation's resources pay for the collective benefit. A brave Australia could make housing a human right and mean it. A brave Australia could lead the climate transition in a way that benefits communities and the planet. A brave Australia could follow through with eliminating poverty. A brave Australia could have politicians who do what is right, even when it's a fight.

Instead of Australia's powerful pulling-back of anyone who sticks their head out of the bucket, a brave Australia would work to help everyone. Even those fighting against it. Centrist politics benefits no one who doesn't already hold power. It proffers aspiration, a modern-day snake oil, while moving the "centre" further and further right, telling you it's always been there.

Big ideas always start small. For Australia to embrace its best self, it just needs some bravery. If politicians and media won't lead the way, then it is up to the people to force it.

Because the thing those in power forget is that truisms are banal. Truths shouldn't need to be sold. They should be innate. And we know when we've been sold a lie. Oftentimes the bravest among us are those who have nothing left to lose. Or in the case of Australia in 2024, those who have never had anything to conserve.

And if the crabs won't let anyone climb out of the bucket, the only thing left to do is kick it over.

Understanding What We Are Up Against

Thomas Mayo

Following the Voice to Parliament Referendum, Aboriginal and Torres Strait Islander people remain as determined as ever to achieve justice and recognition. We will continue to advocate for change because it is necessary for the peace and prosperity of our children, our communities and, in turn, for all Australians. And we know we are far from being alone.

Before the Referendum, Indigenous Australians, who are less than 4% of the population, were working for justice for our people. Now we know that together with our supporters, almost 40% of Australians are striving to achieve this goal.

I believe that the six million Australians who voted "Yes" had cast their ballot with the certainty that they were doing the right thing. On the other hand, the "No" vote was not Australians saying no to Indigenous rights. Many "No" voters want to see a better future for Indigenous children but were confused about how. They were dishonestly told that the Referendum's success would be at their personal cost.

Since the Referendum, some have been using the outcome to argue against any recognition of Indigenous Australia at all, claiming that the "No" vote was a "clear rejection of the Uluru Statement". This is a gross misrepresentation of the Referendum outcome.

And while the enemies of good are seeking to drag us backwards, I am concerned there is now a greater reluctance to demonstrate leadership and vision in Indigenous affairs. While the Albanese government has wasted no time introducing some practical policy advances, such as in Indigenous housing, employment and education, we cannot lose sight of the need for structural and systemic reforms — to address the core of the problem, the torment of our powerlessness.

Facing racism

I first started learning how unfriendly white Australians could be to my people when I was around nine years old. After a wonderful and memorable afternoon at the Darwin Show, my parents, younger sisters and I were driving out of the dusty car park. As we hit the Stuart Highway, a red ute drove alongside us with a group of young white men sitting in the tray. It bewildered and frightened us when, unprovoked, the men spat vile racist abuse at us — "Filthy abos", "Dirty boongs", and worse. Then they sped away.

My strongest memory from the bicentenary year, when I was 11, is another example. Our family was on a long driving holiday, going from Darwin, down the Stuart Highway to Adelaide, and returning home via the east coast. To make the holiday affordable, we would often pull over to cook and eat dinner on the side of the road. Dad would drive through the night, napping in the car if he became too tired, my mum asleep in the front passenger seat and us three kids rugged up in the back. I experienced some of the best of our country on that trip. I also experienced the worst. In a small country town in the south of Queensland, a one-hotel sort of town, the proprietors of the hotel wouldn't serve us. Perhaps we were going to stay in a hotel because Dad was particularly tired that evening. But he drove on. His anger would have kept him awake that night.

Today, as I write this, I have received a text message from an anonymous person who obviously holds strong views about Indigenous Australians. I write it here exactly as it was written.

> if this number is correct it should be thomas mayo . mr mayo , as i live in australia , i know what an australian aboriginals appearance is , and it is not you , david gulpilil yes but not you , i remind you that yes , the fullblood aboriginals were here first , then people from many other nation , then wannabes like you , you and your ilk are a by product of fullbloods and us , so , remember we were here before you (wannabes) . the voice was decided with a NO , you lost , move on

I wouldn't usually share a message like this, though it is one of many. I have received worse: menacing questions about family members and death threats. I felt that sharing this one as an example is important, though, because we need to remove any doubt about how horribly racist some Australians are.

Who Indigenous people are

During the Referendum campaign, it became clear to me that many Australians do not know who Indigenous people are. This unfamiliarity made voters susceptible to the "No" campaign's scare tactics and methods to confuse voters so they would turn against us.

It is easier for a person to believe a vicious rumour about a stranger than about a friend. Familiarity matters. This plays out in the way many Australians are led to believe terrible lies about Aboriginal and Torres Strait Islander people, because in the main, they don't know us.

That we are strangers to most Australians makes sense. As I mentioned earlier, Aboriginal and Torres Strait Islander people make up less than 4% of the population, spread across the vastness of one of the largest countries (by land mass) on Earth. But the reason for the negative and unfriendly views goes much deeper, both historically and as part of the Australian psyche today.

In Noel Pearson's 2022 Boyer Lecture, he mentioned WEH Stanner, a non-Indigenous anthropologist who gave his own Boyer Lectures in 1968. Stanner explained how Australia's sense of its past, its collective memory, had been built on a state of selective forgetfulness that couldn't be "explained by absent-mindedness".

To get his point across he used a powerful analogy showing how ignorance towards Indigenous Australians — our existence, our humanity and our rights — has been by design. Stanner said:

> It is a structural matter, a view from a window which has been carefully placed to exclude a whole quadrant of the landscape. What may well have begun as a simple forgetting of other possible views turned under habit and over time into something like a cult of forgetfulness practised on a national scale.

There are those of us — both Indigenous and non-Indigenous people — who have broken the spell and stepped up to Stanner's window. We have seen a vision of an Australia that includes the perspectives of Aboriginal and Torres Strait Islander people. But we must be aware that the cult of forgetfulness continues, maintained by a few ultra-conservative historians, shock-jock radio commentators, columnists and TV hosts, and it has a real effect on the psyche of many of the people we love.

These immoral influencers have made a career from a niche in the media that exploits how little Australians know about Indigenous people. They exaggerate, misinform and use fallacies to generate clicks, to create fear. They loudly ask questions without accepting the answers that come from Indigenous leaders and eminent legal authorities. Most egregiously, they lie when they claim that Indigenous people want Australians' personal property, especially their land.

When people are told to mistrust Aboriginal and Torres Strait Islander people, and when combined with the deep-seated amnesia that Stanner speaks of, it is more likely these people will resist change.

The Referendum was an opportunity for voters to face up to the past and present injustices. And many responded positively. There were valuable, open conversations that I and many supporters enjoyed across the country. But the cult of forgetfulness and fearmongering continued its work — the result was that people were angry at us. Such strong feelings were certainly felt at the polling booths.

The greatest challenge in achieving justice for Indigenous Australians is twofold. First, we need to understand the inherent prejudice that will take a strong and united effort to overcome. Secondly, we need to help fair-minded Australians become familiar with the truth of who we First Peoples are.

We must use truth to protect our fellow Australians from the lies they will continue to hear.

In any analysis of the Referendum, whether in a conversation at home or at work, or in an article, book or essay you might read, it may be that you agree with arguments about flaws in the "Yes" campaign;

you may speculate on what the Prime Minister could have done differently; or in hindsight, you might believe we should have waited for more favourable economic times.

While all aspects of the attempted constitutional recognition of the First Peoples is fair game, we should always remember that the most significant factor that turned Australians from a majority who would vote "Yes" in the early polls, into a majority who voted "No", were the powerful few — the Bad Actors — who chose to use the Referendum as a weapon in their ideological wars against peace and justice in our country.

We should also remember that a vast majority of Indigenous communities voted "Yes".

This is an amended extract from Thomas Mayo's *Always Was, Always Will Be: The campaign for justice and recognition continues*, published by Hardie Grant Books in September 2024.

Three Things You Need to Know About Climate Change

Dr Joëlle Gergis

The thing that frustrates me most about the climate change "debate" is how much time we think we have left to avert planetary scale disaster. As one of the climate scientists involved in the United Nations' Intergovernmental Panel on Climate Change (IPCC) *Sixth Assessment Report*, I understand that every day we delay, we are baking in more warming that has the power to unlock irreversible climate change that will be impossible to adapt to. Because scientists are expected to remain apolitical, to not jeopardise our professional reputation and government funding, most people steer clear of political conversations that might see our objectivity questioned. This means that the public doesn't hear enough from the people who know most about the reality we are facing. Many experts are also afraid of inviting trouble their way: when you speak out, you become a target for personal attacks that can derail your career, with little to no institutional support to help weather the storms.

Given how rapidly the crisis is escalating, the price of silence now feels intolerable. In 1959 Martin Luther King summarised the harm of political apathy by saying: "If you fail to act now, history will have to record that the greatest tragedy of this period of social transition was not the strident clamour of the bad people, but the appalling silence of the good people."

So, in the spirit of being on the right side of history, here are three key things that scientists like me want you to know about climate change. The first is that the situation is bad. Worse than you think. Right now, the Earth is on track for a catastrophic overshooting of the Paris Agreement target of limiting warming to under 2°C above pre-industrial levels. As things stand, there is a 90% chance that current climate policies will see the world warm by 2.3°C to 4.5°C by the end of the century, with a best estimate of 3.5°C. Even if all net zero pledges made under the Paris Agreement are met, we are still looking at global warming of between 2 and 3°C by 2100, with a best estimate of 2.4°C.

As a reminder, global average temperatures have already increased by approximately 1.2°C above pre-industrial levels, so we are essentially on track for three times the warming we've already experienced. This means the environmental destruction and societal disruption we have witnessed so far will continue to compound and dwarf anything we have experienced throughout the entire course of human history. Of particular concern is the fact that we now know that abrupt climate change can be triggered at lower levels of global warming, meaning that it is possible that the Earth will experience major transformations even if we manage to achieve the goals of the Paris Agreement. The latest research shows that several tipping points, such as the disintegration of the West Antarctic and Greenland ice sheets, may be triggered within the Paris Agreement range of 1.5°C to 2°C of global warming. For context, if the West Antarctic ice sheet melts, there is the potential for the global sea level to rise by around 4 metres, with an additional 7 metres held in Greenland. The problem is that once you melt an ice sheet, you can't get that genie back in the bottle — it takes thousands of years to refreeze, so you can think of sea-level rise as irreversible on timescales of tens of thousands of years. According to the latest IPCC report, the world is committed to 2 to 3 metres of global sea-level rise over coming centuries even if warming is limited to 1.5°C, rising to up to 6 metres with 2°C of peak warming. As a rule of thumb, coastal experts estimate that every 1-metre rise in sea level results in a 100-metre retreat of the coastline. Most people don't truly fathom the scale of the destruction we face even with 1.5°C, let alone the planetary reconfiguration that will occur if we fail to reduce emissions and warm our world by 3.5°C by the end of this century. So, in a nutshell, the reality we need to face here is that it will not be possible to adapt to such high levels of global warming. In fact, it is delusional and dangerous to pretend that we can.

The second thing scientists want you to know is that the situation is going to get worse. The net zero pledges world governments have committed to rely heavily on the use of carbon capture and storage (CCS) technology. This means that industrial polluters like coal- or gas-fired plants can continue on with business as usual, as long as they say they will have a CCS attached to their operations to "abate" their emissions. Essentially CCS involves condensing carbon emissions into a liquid which is then injected deep underground or offshore into "permanent" geologic storage.

Although CCS might sound like a good idea in theory, the true risks of the hazards associated with the CCS industry are yet to be fully scientifically and technically assessed, let alone comprehensively regulated. The other problem is that in practice, CCS doesn't work at the scale required to significantly reduce global emissions. According to the United Nations Environment Programme, around 80% of pilot CCS projects have failed over the past 30 years, with operational facilities storing less than 10 million tonnes of carbon dioxide per year. However, according to the Global CCS Institute industry group, in 2023 there were 41 commercial CCS plants worldwide capable of capturing 49 million tonnes of carbon dioxide each year. If we compare the 49 million tonnes sequestered by CCS to the record high 40.6 billion tonnes of carbon dioxide the world burnt through in 2023, currently operational carbon capture plants are only able to offset approximately 0.1% of global carbon emissions. In other words, CCS technology is currently only offsetting one-tenth of 1% of total global emissions emitted each year. Using carbon capture technology to justify the continued burning of fossil fuels is an unforgiveable betrayal of future generations that will guarantee the destabilisation of the Earth's climate.

The third thing I'd like you to know is that our political leaders still aren't doing enough to address the crisis. Despite stated climate pledges, governments all over the world are still planning to produce more than double the amount of fossil fuels in 2030 than is consistent with limiting warming to 1.5°C. Collectively, there are plans to increase global coal production until 2030 and oil and gas reserves until at least 2050, despite many major producer countries pledging net zero emissions targets by mid-century. According to the International Monetary Fund, in 2022 world governments spent around $7 trillion on fossil fuel subsidies, while here in Australia, in 2023–2024 state and federal governments provided $14.5 billion to support heavy polluters. Despite all the lip service and all that is at stake, our political leaders are still choosing to prop up an industry that we know is cooking the planet.

As a climate scientist, it's becoming increasingly hard to know what to say about the mess we are now in. As someone who understands that we are witnessing the destabilisation of the Earth's climate, remaining silent no longer feels like an option. We know that 82% of carbon dioxide emissions since 1960 have come from the burning of coal, oil and gas, and that their rapid elimination is needed to avoid irreversible changes to our planet. While I understand that shutting down the fossil-fuel industry is politically difficult, I can assure you that trying to "adapt" to an uninhabitable world will be infinitely harder.

Every day we delay, the more permanent changes we lock into the climate system. Our leaders need to have the guts to put a price on carbon and accelerate the clean energy transition as fast as is humanly possible. And we, as citizens, need to keep the political pressure on our leaders to do better and enact science-based climate policies to secure a liveable future. If we fail to rise to this challenge, people in the future will look back at the world's collective failure to shut down the fossil fuel industry during the 2020s and see it for what it really was — an intergenerational crime against humanity.

A Radical Act of Diplomacy

Professor Clare Wright OAM

In hindsight, the question was revolutionary.

Upending my world view was not on my mind when I posed the question. Not exactly spur of the moment or throwaway — I'd been curious — but my intent in making the enquiry was to scratch an itch, not open a flesh wound.

Nha Yolŋu yaku for Bark Petition? I asked the man sitting beside me in the passenger seat one muggy tropical morning as we drove to his wife's funeral in Gunyaŋara, a remote community in north-east Arnhem Land.

Seven words. Four of them in a language I barely spoke; three in my mother tongue.

"What is the Yolŋu word for Bark Petition?"

The man stared at me in stony silence. Clearly he'd never been asked this question before. Ḏäku dhäruk, he slowly replied.

Ḏäku, the bark of the local gadayka tree, the canvas on which Yolŋu paintings are made.

Dhäruk, the word, the message. A meeting from which a message comes.

Boom.

The outsized concept that Galarrwuy Yunupingu, leader of the Gumatj clan of the Yolŋu people, former Chairman of the Northern Land Council, Australian of the Year, elder statesman in two worlds, dropped in my lap on that steamy day of sorry business in 2020 arrived with the force of thunder. Galarrwuy and I had been discussing a history of the Yirrkala Bark Petitions for over five years already. I hadn't seen this coming.

The "Bark Petitions" was what the documents tended to the Australian federal Parliament in August 1963, signed by 12 members of the Yolŋu people, protesting against the incursion of mining interests on their land, had come to be colloquially known. It's the term you'll find at Parliament House, where the two petitions presented to the House of Representatives are on permanent display. It's the term you'll find in books about the history of land rights in Australia, where the Bark Petitions receive an obligatory nod as the progenitors of Mabo. It's the term you'll find on the National Museum of Australia's Defining Moments Digital Classroom, tucked in on a timeline between 1962 (Indigenous Australians granted the right to vote) and 1966 (end of the White Australia Policy). It's the term you'll find if you ask Google what was the first petition put to the Australian Parliament in an Australian language.

"Bark Petitions" is the term used to describe the four artefacts which are part traditional Westminster-style paper petition, employing the formal wording of any request to parliament following standing orders — "the humble petition of the undersigned" ... "and your petitioners as in duty bound will ever pray God to help you and us" — and part traditional bark paintings, employing the symbols and designs which convey the laws of the land on which the Yolŋu people had lived and had held in custody for tens of thousands of years; since "the time before morning".

It was not until I asked Galarrwuy what the Yolŋu people called these famed objects that it started to dawn on me that the "Bark Petitions" were not petitions at all.

When the Menzies government excised 140 square miles of land from the Arnhem Land Reserve in April 1963, having granted leases to extract bauxite to a French mining company two months earlier, the seventeen Yolŋu clans of the Miwatj region (Gove Peninsula) had no reason to believe that they were not the sovereign owners of their tribal lands. The Macassan fisherman who had been coming to their shores for at least five centuries had respectfully abided by Yolŋu laws of the land. Yolŋu had warded off the colonial pastoralists; in Arnhem Land, the "black wars" of the 19th century were won by the blacks. Japanese pearlers had felt the sharp end of the sword of Yolŋu justice when rules of engagement were transgressed in the early 20th century. Members of the RAAF who were stationed in the region in World War II came and went, leaving only an airstrip. Methodist missionaries who had set up a station at Yirrkala in 1935 had learned to speak the language, condoned the continuation of hunting and ceremony and, apart from the encouragement to come to church on Sunday and for children to go to school, had otherwise made no demands on Yolŋu who voluntarily came from their homelands to live at the mission. Yolŋu graciously offered their hospitality, and the missionaries knew they were but guests.

The spectre of dispossession came late to Arnhem Land by virtue of the extractive frontier. Bauxite wasn't discovered until the late 1950s. By 1963, sensing a new kind of danger, the clans of the region put aside their own historic hostilities and determined to speak in one voice against the new common enemy. Outsiders had broken Yolŋu law by failing to consult before coming on to the land, neither seeking consent to take resources nor offering compensation for their potential removal.

It was a visiting opposition Labor MP, Kim Beazley, in Yirrkala in July 1963 on a fact-finding mission (after the mission's superintendent, Rev Edgar Wells, blew the whistle on Menzies) who suggested expressing these collective clan grievances by way of a formal petition. He gave Yolŋu leaders the requisite parliamentary language and the novel suggestion of pasting the petition onto bark.

Overnight, four such petitions were painted, frames on which to adhere the written petition. The paintings flouted Yolŋu convention by mixing moieties, combining Dhuwa and Yirritja sacred designs, to present a cohesive narrative of belonging, a proprietary claim of geographical and cosmological location. The story told in the paintings was simple yet existential: we are here, this land is our land, our voices must be heard.

Not a petition. Not a bottom-up plea from a downtrodden people to a higher power. Not a humble entreaty from a supplicant to someone in a position of superior power and authority. The people with this brand-new pan-Yolŋu identity respected the Australian government's protocols — collectively choosing its most literate representatives, nine young men and three young women who had had sufficient mission education to sign their names — and communicating the truth of their own laws in the language of both the Australians (English) and traditional owners (Yolŋu Matha).

They sent a dhäruk. A message. A material emissary. Bark envoys, hewn from the trees that were earthly ancestors as much as arboreal assets. The political relationship expressed was not hierarchical, but horizontal. One sovereign nation's gift to another. The agreement sought was a negotiated detente, not a prayer for mercy. The words written at the top — "the humble petition of the Undersigned aboriginal people of Yirrkala" — were just as meaningless, as incomprehensible, to the Yolŋu as the paintings were to the Australians.

That the Bark Petitions "failed" to elicit any of the consultation, consent or compensation that the Yolŋu leaders and their white allies sought rested as much on the Australian leaders' sheer incapacity to read the message as their unwillingness to heed it.

It was the Menzies government that failed to appreciate the gesture of goodwill, failed to reciprocate the respect afforded by the Yolŋu to the Australian legal and political system.

Far from being "humble", the Yirrkala Bark Petitions radically transfigure Western timelines of progress and development precisely because they suggest the pre-existence of sophisticated systems of government on the Australian continent prior to European settlement/invasion. The legal fiction of terra nullius did not only pertain to land tenure; it also assumes the continent was void of governance.

As we begin to fathom the ecological extent of "deep time", we also need to appreciate the depth of technocratic time on this island continent.

The assertion of ancient Indigenous lineage in Western concepts and practices (agriculture, astronomy, design, scientific innovation) has recently gained a footing in literature and theory. What about politics? "The art of the possible" as Germany's elder statesman Otto von Bismarck would have it, "the art of the next best"?

Arguably, there are parallels between Indigenous political philosophy and political economy and democratic principles of power-sharing. (Governance relied upon processes of delegated decision-making, but male elders determined who the delegates, including women, would be.) Yolŋu society was certainly not despotic, totalitarian or tyrannical. Decisions about how the people were to be ordered, managed and led were made by community representatives (rom waŋaŋu walal), through "parliaments" (ŋärra), via rules encoded in a "constitution" (dhulma-mulka bathi). Relationships of foreign affairs and trade were expressed and policed through contracts (djugu'-gurrupan) and systems of return payment (buku-bakmaram). Designated areas (riŋgitj wäŋa) were demarcated for the negotiation of ingress onto another clan's land. Legal instruments gave representatives power and authority (ganydjarr) to seek compensation for trespass onto land or theft of resources. The goal of good governance was to create a state of equality and harmony (mägaya), a state of peace, justice and freedom from hostilities. The entire system of governance, jurisprudence, commerce and industry was based on Yolŋu law (maŋayin).

When that law needed to be communicated to the Australian nation, "the land grew a tongue". The message was written on a bark.

With the words ŋäku dhäruk now in white Australia's political lexicon, the Yirrkala Bark Petitions demonstrate the political sophistication of a people engaging in acts of statesmanship between two nations by attempting to speak in one unifying idiom: the language of diplomacy.

The Yolŋu authors/artists of the Bark Petitions were not humble petitioners; they were self-assured political leaders reaching out to fellow politicians, certain in the knowledge that their sovereignty had never and could never be ceded.

Like Ŋäku Dhäruk/the Bark Petitions, the Uluru Statement from the Heart offers an invitation for settler Australia and the nation's First People to walk together towards a future in which today's parliamentary leaders might learn to listen to, learn from and respect the voice of those Indigenous leaders who have, for over 60 years, been reaching out across the linguistic and epistemological divide. Our robust, relevant democracy requires no less.

Frameworks of Insecurity

President José Ramos-Horta

Language is a truly fascinating phenomenon. I myself speak five languages fluently: Tetum (the native language of Timor-Leste), Portuguese, French, English and Spanish.

Language is fluid and constantly evolving. But we are barely aware that, as we are shaping its evolution, language is shaping us — individually and collectively. This is what makes it such a potent political tool.

Language can be a tool of liberation and empowerment. It can also be a tool of suppression and control.

The political curation of language — repetition of words, the stripping of their nuance, sharpening or distorting of their definition and even their complete erasure — can influence a national psyche just as effectively as weapons.

With just a few keystrokes governments, corporations and the media can dramatically shift public sentiment against democratic participants: transforming a "protestor" into an "extremist", an "independent critic" into an "activist", a "refugee" into an "illegal".

These powerful actors can similarly edit the national lexicon to influence public understanding of their own actions. I have seen first-hand how "inequality" and "extreme wealth" has been explained as a manifestation of "freedom". How "authoritarianism" has been rebranded as "social cohesion".

"Human rights violations", "surveillance", "political machismo", "oppression" no longer exist in some places. To be clear, the actions are still very much there, they have just been rendered as nameless, necessary components of maintaining social order and, of course, "security".

This term, "security", has been a pervasive and recurring presence in my life over the last 50 or so years, and my observation is that the political manipulation of this word has profoundly influenced human interactions, attitudes and collective psychology.

A noun once synonymous with peace, safety and harmony is now implicitly threatening. It accommodates traditional discourse of war and conflict without the need to refer directly to them. "Security" has been militarised and mobilised, somehow more verb than noun. "Security" is something that can be inflicted upon people in various ways: posturing, intimidation, withholding support, diplomatic silence or physical acts of hostility.

All manner of domestic and international transgressions are now seemingly acts of "security".

And we are told that these acts are necessary to deal with the ever-present threats to our security lurking at the fringes of our lives — even if we can't see them — because those at the top are privy to information and intelligence that we are not.

We have been led to believe that "security", as it pertains to national and international frameworks, is something deeply technical that only the institutional elite understand and have access to, so we are told not question it.

If we did, we might wonder why protestors blocking traffic, or whistleblowers exposing the crimes of government, or any aspect of the People's Republic of China you might care to name, are treated as more sinister and urgent threats to global security than the climate change, floods and deadly heat, hunger, poverty, child malnutrition, gender violence and disregard for international law we are either witnessing or experiencing every day.

In my roles as an activist, a politician, a scholar in peace studies and international law, a Nobel Laureate and a UN Special Envoy I have always advocated strenuously for the simplest, most universal and human interpretation of security.

The vast majority of what is being carried out in the name of national, regional or international security, are actually textbook expressions of deep-rooted insecurity, motivated by insecurity and designed to maintain insecurity.

If "security" as it is currently practised were accurately renamed to reflect this, it would be far easier to see it for what it was. Not a means to achieve peace or stability within nations or between them, but a tool of subjugation to serve the interests and egos of a small number of powerful actors. To keep citizens perpetually fearful, suspicious and strategically compliant.

But it will never achieve this goal either. While subjugation might result in silence or order, vaguely resembling security from a distance, let me tell you that silence and order is only ever temporary. And one doesn't need to be a Nobel laureate or expert in international law to know this.

Ask yourself, how much long-term success would a parent have in nurturing their relationship with their child using threats, suspicion and violence? How much long-term success would an employer have running a harmonious workplace using surveillance and coercion? How much long-term success would a spouse have maintaining a secure marriage that has been built on leveraging power?

I am not the first to ponder the evolving definition of security. But I want to be clear that, while I am writing in general terms to make a point, there is nothing hypothetical or abstract in my words. I am only tenuously interested in the role of security in political theory. Of far greater interest to me is the very real impact the interpretation and transmission of this word by political actors has on the lives of people, including those in Australia and my people in Timor-Leste.

I am one of the few people alive in the world who can say they have been instrumental in building a democracy. Not just from the ground up, but painstakingly and precariously from scorched earth up. And I can tell you that security is something that must come from within. Whether in the context of an individual or a nation-state, to be at peace with others, we must be at peace with ourselves.

When people are genuinely secure in their identity, when they are emotionally and physically secure, they maintain their independence while cultivating a generosity of spirit. The welfare of others is not a threat to their own. In fact, the opposite is true: when others are similarly nourished and secure, what manifests is collective peace and trust. They thrive together.

Conversely, as I suggest above, those who are insecure, who have no sense of self, are jealous and easily threatened. They are fearful, harbour grievances and are prone to lashing out. Insecurity breeds collective distrust, dysfunction and an inability to respect boundaries. I say this as the president of a country still healing from the direct, lived experience of others' insecurity — including those we called allies.

However, Timor-Leste has made the conscious decision not to perpetuate the cycle of insecurity inflicted upon us, and while we are by no means perfect, we are a nation at peace with ourselves, our neighbours and the world.

Timor-Leste is also consciously committed to the concept of real security: collective safety, prosperity and harmony. Years of foreign occupation and the path we forged to independence makes us uniquely qualified to know that the most efficient and effective and morally tenable way to achieve real security is by helping each other to flourish.

As the United Nations Secretary-General António Guterres has said, "Timor-Leste demonstrated that nothing solid or lasting can be built on the denial of people's fundamental rights … The world can learn much from Timor-Leste, especially at a time when conflicts are multiplying and geopolitical tensions are worsening. And in a context of worrying dysfunctionality in the relationship between powers and growing impunity in the face of violations of human rights and international law."

While finding its feet as one of the world's youngest democracies, Timor-Leste has also been mindful of its role as a global citizen, contributing personnel to United Nations peacekeeping missions since 2011, including in Kosovo, Lebanon, South Sudan and Guinea-Bissau. Timor-Leste established and chairs the G7+, a coalition of 18 fragile and conflict-affected nations from around the globe. In 2022 Timor-Leste gave over AUD$2.2 million in humanitarian aid to the Ukraine.

Despite our best efforts, Timor-Leste continues to be under resourced and underdeveloped and is described as one of the world's "poorest" countries. We have made tremendous progress on health and education and social development, but we will not fully achieve or contribute meaningfully to real security without real support. It is entirely reasonable to expect the larger, richer countries that have historically built their wealth off colonisation and exploitation of countries like mine to do this, not as reparations or even charity, but out of economic pragmatism.

That is, when Australia looks at Timor-Leste and Pacific Island countries, it should view them as extensions of its own national security interests. The peace and prosperity of Australia is not only dependent on having healthy, secure citizens within its borders, but a stable, peaceful and prosperous region more broadly.

Instead, the value governments place on insecurity is reflected in the vast amounts of money they spend on propaganda, conflict, weapons and military posturing every year. In fact, globally, more money than ever before is being spent on the military, which would appear to confirm that current frameworks of national and international "security", as defined by the global elite, are better at feeding insecurity than ameliorating it.

In 2023, military spending worldwide was AUD$3.5 trillion — the highest amount ever spent and a figure so big it is meaningless to most of us. By contrast, in the same year, money spent by governments globally on official development assistance (ODA) such as health and education and infrastructure in developing countries was AUD$332 billion (less than 10% of military spending).

Australia is Timor-Leste's most significant development and "security" partner. Our countries share a long and complex history and Australia contributes significantly to Timor-Leste's development through official development assistance and other support in recognition of this relationship. But again, the value Australia places on insecurity is far more than it places on collective peace and prosperity despite significant rhetoric suggesting otherwise.

The Australian government claims to be delivering just over AUD$2.1 billion in total ODA to Pacific Island countries (including Timor-Leste which will be allocated around AUD$123 million) in 2024–25. This is not insubstantial.

But it is also best viewed in context. In the same year the Australian government has committed AUD$2.6 billion to its famous nuclear submarines. This is also roughly the same amount as Timor-Leste's total annual public expenditure on all government services. Tell me, which is a better investment? The mental and physical health and subsequent loyalty of your allies? Or weapons that I hear will not even belong to your country if they are ever built.

While I am told Australia's development assistance has and will continue to decline under your current budget settings, funding for defence will reach AUD$765 billion over this decade.

It is simply not tenable for Australians or the Timorese to thrive under this model of national or regional "security". Australia and Timor-Leste are interdependent. I can tell you with absolute certainty that insecurity in both our countries will only grow under the current trajectory.

If we cannot change the word "security", then we must reclaim ownership of its definition. We must question the activities carried out in its name. We must insist on our participation in it because it is our security.

To be secure is to thrive. To be safe. To be free. All of us.

A version of this essay first appeared in *The Saturday Paper*.

National Power, Agency and a Foreign Policy that Delivers

Allan Behm

Not quite 80 years ago, Hans Morgenthau published his magisterial *Politics Among Nations*. A ground-breaking analysis of what constitutes national power, Morgenthau explained America's rise to global dominance. But he also described the template that enabled the nations smashed by the horrors of World War II — victors and vanquished alike — to rebuild. Britain was bankrupt. France was deeply divided and about to embark on disastrous post-colonial wars. Germany was divided and had effectively ceased to exist as a state, as had Japan. China was reeling from nearly two decades of civil war, and the Soviet Union's victory in eastern Europe had come at vast social and economic cost.

Only America emerged from World War II with its national power enhanced, thereby affording it the agency to build a post-World War II world in its own image and based on rules largely designed and operated as an artefact of the American imperium.

Fast forward to the present and a very different power distribution is in play. The US remains top dog, largely by virtue of its military power, though it finds it difficult to come to terms with the fact that "power" is not univocal. Power takes many forms, and the immense cultural power that largely defines China and Russia is something that America finds difficult to contemplate, much less accommodate. And for the countries that constitute the G20, the combinations and variations of the elements of national power have established their identities in large measure and determine their agency as independent and collaborative global players.

Australia is no exception.

By any measure, Australia enjoys considerable national power. The constant retreat into the sham comfort of "middle power" (as though we were an antipodean version of the Baltic states) and "punching above our weight" represents a serious failure of confidence, imagination and political leadership. We occupy a continent. Our resource base is practically limitless. Our economy currently ranks 12th, perhaps just in front of Russia in current circumstances. On some calculations, four of our capital cities are in the top hundred in terms of amenity and habitability. On other measures, eight of our universities are in the top hundred global tertiary institutions — a remarkable achievement for a population of 26 million.

Even in terms of military spending, Australia ranks 13th in the world — albeit a long way behind the US and China. On Morgenthau's reckoning, we are a well-educated society demonstrating high levels of acceptance and inclusion, though always capable of improvement of course, as the failure of the Voice Referendum demonstrated only too starkly. Australia also boasts a robust health and social security system with strong safety nets across the entire population. This is what 21st century power looks like.

Yet when it comes to the exercise of national power — performing as a constructive and independent actor on the global stage — Australia is defensive, uncertain and timid. On what we like to describe as "strategic" matters (though we do not seem to have much of an idea of what a strategic issue really is), we fall in behind America and, amazingly, Great Britain, and take comfort from fictions like the Quad where India's and Japan's roles are ambiguous, to say the least. We are constantly embarrassed in our dealings with our Asian neighbours, at once condescending and culturally uncomprehending.

For all our fear of the so-called threat from China in the Pacific, we retreat behind platitudes like "our Pacific family" but remain tight-fisted when it comes to constructive economic development. To take just one example: the paucity of health services in the Pacific, especially for women and children, is nothing short of a national disgrace for a wealthy country that claims to care about its neighbours. Papua New Guinea's health system is on the verge of collapse, and instead of offering financial and medical support, we lecture PNG on governance. Really?

There are some deep pathologies that constrain Australia's agency. For all our protestations to the contrary, we are widely seen in Asia and the Pacific as deeply racist, and we are. Again, just contemplate the Voice Referendum. We are a structurally misogynistic society, with male entitlement continuing to dominate business and the professions. We are insecure, afraid of abandonment and constantly in search of reassurance from a great and powerful protector. And we are diffident in our ability to self-affirm, always looking for American or British approval.

There is, however, a remedy to these constraints on our national agency, and the remedy is well within our grasp if only we were to draw on our considerable national power. And what is the key to mobilising the elements of national power and creating agency? As Morgenthau pointed out, agency comes into its own when the quality of a nation's diplomacy combines the elements of national power into an integrated whole, giving them direction and weight.

Australia conducts its foreign policy in fits and starts,

alternating initial enthusiasm with a reluctance to sustain delivery. Foreign Ministers such as Doc Evatt, Percy Spender, Gough Whitlam, Andrew Peacock, Gareth Evans and more recently Penny Wong have shown what can be done when there is clarity of purpose and drive. Yet a successful and sustained diplomacy takes more than ambition and imagination. It takes resources, which we are simply unwilling to allocate. There is bipartisan support for a Defence budget of just under $60 billion per annum, while the DFAT allocation on diplomacy is just over $1.8 billion — less than half the allocation to Official Development Assistance at $4.2 billion. Notwithstanding its fatuous and oft-repeated claim to "punch above its weight", Australia ranks 26th on the Global Diplomacy Index and within the G20 it fields the second smallest diplomatic network. And as the global south expands in power and influence, Australia is barely visible in Africa, the Americas, the Middle East and Central Asia. Complacency is a sure track to irrelevance.

Successive governments have talked about disruption and uncertainty, mostly in response to China's economic growth. Yet our response to that disruption and uncertainty is not to increase our diplomatic effort but to acquire long-range nuclear-powered submarines that may never materialise, while we hunker down behind nervous disengagement. If we are serious about the need for a global rules-based order that it is not just an artefact of the Pax Americana but a genuinely inclusive approach to human wellbeing and global prosperity, we need to practise our advocacy everywhere, not just where we feel comfortable.

We have the national power to do this, just as we have the key elements of diplomatic agency. But we need the policies and funding to perform a more active and engaged internationalist role.

In Defence of Public Broadcasting

Alex Sloan AM

"I think the ABC is finished." I heard these words over dinner, separately said by two incredibly smart, hardworking friends: one a senior academic, the other an author of more than a dozen books and chief executive of a leading national organisation. They are in the business of thinking, of knowing.

This opinion that our public broadcaster is finished or that it's "not what it was" is expressed a lot these days. No doubt you're thinking of your latest gripe; I know I have my own. But I also know that we would be a different country without the ABC. As *The Sydney Morning Herald* noted when the ABC turned 75 — you would still have an Australia without the ABC, but it wouldn't be this Australia.

Former ABC MD Mark Scott reminded us in 2015, when the then latest ridiculous overblown firestorm erupted asking the ABC "whose side was it on?", that he often had to remind politicians "that they do seem to get obsessed about 2% of the ABC's content — usually the part that's about them or the issues their polling currently says is important". He went on to say: "the ABC is for all Australians and it's much bigger and broader and richer than that".

Think Bluey, health, science, education, entertainment, sport, local and regional programming and emergency broadcasting into every nook and cranny of the Australian community. That's just a tiny snapshot of the content that is delivered on radio, TV and online every day. All this programming while there have been savage cuts to the ABC's budget: big bucks, nearly a billion dollars in cuts over 10 years.

A slashed budget and the loss of hundreds of senior journalists; does anyone think the cuts and political attacks won't have an impact? And let's not forget the deliberate stacking of the ABC board by federal governments with their mates. They all do it.

So, what's the alternative to a publicly funded, accountable broadcaster, which contributes to the health of democracy, helping to keep people well-informed, politically engaged and socially cohesive?

At the same time, Australian commercial media is so desperately concerned with its own survival, it publishes hundreds of articles attacking the ABC. One commercial outlet was so intent on securing what they described as "the most amazing thing on Australian TV ever"— an interview with an accused rapist — that it spent hundreds of thousands of dollars on renting a fancy apartment, sex workers, cocaine, boys' golfing trips to Tasmania and something called a Tomahawk steak.

And then we have the mega players. Social media. Two out of every five Australians now nominate social media as their main source of news, and that number is even higher among young adults.

Social media companies source news content wherever they can find it. In Australia a deal was done which saw Australian news publishers paid about $70 million a year for content. This deal is now off. Facebook along with other global tech giants use and monetise Australian news content on their platforms. It does not matter if this content is factual; it matters if a lot of people consume it. Facebook owner Meta is estimated to be worth $1.9 trillion dollars.

Rough estimates have Meta earning between $2 and $5 billion a year in Australia and paying little if no tax.

There is a lot of money in disinformation and universities are also on the frontline. A case against Harvard University is underway, brought by their former online disinformation researcher who has accused the university of pushing her out and shutting down her work to shield the school's relationship with Facebook owner Meta, which has pledged US$500 million to the university. The complainant, Joan Donovan, alleges her involvement in a project to publish thousands of internal Facebook documents leaked by former Facebook employee turned whistleblower, Frances Haugen, was the trigger that led Harvard to shut down her work and ultimately eliminate her role.

So, let me leave you with my response to the "ABC is finished" line by returning to the aim of public broadcasting. The Public Media Alliance, the largest global association of public service broadcasters, has this to say:

> The main purpose of public media is to provide a variety of quality content that is universally accessible to a diverse audience on a national level. This includes providing reliable information to the public so that they can participate in society in a meaningful way, such as rigorous and impartial election coverage, while a number of public media also play a critical role in public service messaging during emergencies and crises. Impartial domestic and international news coverage is also central to Public Service Media in order to inform public understanding of a complex and globalised world.

Over the past five years, repeated surveys have come up with the same answer to the question: "To what extent does a nation's democratic health relate to the strength of its public service media?"

Democratic values in countries with a weak public service media (PSM) decline. Citizens are more satisfied with democracy in countries with well-funded PSM; the higher the PSM TV market shares, the less citizens think of authoritarian leadership as a good way of governing. Citizens trust one another more in countries where the position of PSM is strong. The more well-funded a PSM is, the more citizens feel confident of being able to participate in politics.

Our public broadcaster is a precious and vital part of Australian life and culture and it's front and centre in maintaining the health of our democracy. It can't be cowed by political and competitor pressure. It needs a board and management who stand up to this pressure, who fight for a strong public broadcaster because that fight is a fight for our democracy.

Doing Politics Differently: Safeguarding Australian Democracy

Alana Johnson AM

"The epic political challenge of the 21st century is not only to show democracy still works but also to keep democracy alive as the functioning model of our contemporary societies"[1] writes veteran journalist Paul Kelly.

As the hyper-partisan United States descends into politically motivated violence and other established democracies such as Hungary, Poland, Turkey and Israel are eroding democratic norms, a quiet political transformation is occurring in Australia — a people's movement to reclaim democracy and place communities at the centre of politics.

At the 2022 federal election Community Independent candidates were elected in the seats of Kooyong, Mackellar, Wentworth, Goldstein, North Sydney and Curtin, joining the members for Indi and Warringah on the largest ever crossbench in the history of the House of Representatives. The ACT also voted in the first Community Independent to the Senate.

While the election of these independents might have taken the apparatchiks of the major parties by surprise, the election result was an outcome of a community-led movement that began ten years earlier.

In 2012 a dozen ordinary people in north-east Victoria came together — driven by despair about how their community was being represented in Parliament — to reimagine their democracy. Through shared values and a desire to elevate the voices of their regional communities, these citizens formed Voices for Indi.

With an innovative grassroots campaign and the selection of Cathy McGowan as their independent candidate, the people of Indi delivered the Coalition its only loss of a sitting member in the 2013 election, as a blue wave washed over the nation.

Indi made history again in 2019 when the people elected Helen Haines to become the first Independent in the federal Parliament to succeed a retiring Independent MP. Concurrently, a community-led campaign saw Zali Steggall elected the Independent Member for Warringah.

Through values-based, respectful processes, nine communities have found electoral success, rewriting the political playbook and inspiring a nationwide Community Independents movement.

More than 20,000 people were involved in the 2022 independent campaigns, and currently there are almost 50 electoral community groups, reimagining Voices for Indi and meeting across the nation. A new form of political engagement is sweeping the country with people from 125 (of 151) federal electorates participating in the 2024 Community Independents Project convention.

The citizens at the heart of the Community Independents movement are reclaiming democracy and forging a new relationship dynamic between themselves and their elected representatives.

The restoration of a workable representative democracy in Australia is predicated on simple, time-honoured ideas: electing members of Parliament who are committed to knowing their constituents' views, who speak on their behalf and are accountable to them for how they represent them. It doesn't sound radical — but the lack of representation in our representative democracy is no longer being accepted.

Public trust has been battered by partisan politicians putting party, donors and their own career advancement ahead of the needs of the people they represent. Long duped into accepting "this is how politics works", citizens are finding their political awakening in a movement that is doing politics differently.

We do not need to redesign Parliament or do away with political parties. What Australian democracy needs is a shift in the power dynamic, a change in the relationship between citizens and their elected representatives. Australians are fed up with a system of government that vests power in opaque party machines, career politicians, big business, and powerful corporate interests. The Community Independent movement presents a different, more active style of citizenship, resulting in a different, more engaged type of politician.

It is a universal truth that listening is a powerful gift, one that is deeply validating for the oft unheard person sharing their views. Respectfully hearing views builds trust, people find common ground, and both parties learn how to disagree constructively. Listening enhances inclusion and belonging.

The Victorian Women's Trust[2] designed a model of civic engagement known as Kitchen Table Conversations which has been adopted and adapted by community electoral groups to give people from all walks of life a voice and an invitation to participate in their democracy.

It is a defining feature of the Community Independents movement that independent candidates are identified, assessed and selected by local people, rather than through entrenched party processes or by self-selection.

Being nominated and elected as a Community Independent

means accepting a compact to establish a genuine two-way collaborative process with the community. The MP continually seeks to understand the views of their community and the constituents actively engage and collaborate with the MP in return. This form of civic engagement can be expressed in many forms: town hall meetings, deliberative forums, street meets, constituent volunteers in electorate offices and Parliament House, policy advisory groups, and any number of ways to give people a voice in their democracy. The social compact is the motivating factor of a Community Independent campaign that mobilises thousands of active citizens to turn up, to participate, to build connection and to find a common purpose underpinned by shared values.

There is an expectation of all those involved to "be the change you want to see happen". Restoring decency, respect and integrity to Parliament is central to the Community Independents movement. Signing up to these values means there is no place for negativity or slagging off political opponents. This expectation extends to the Community Independent MPs once elected, which has influenced a positive shift in the behaviour of MPs in the House of Representatives.

Australian democracy has been stuck in a cycle of divisive adversarial politics riddled with inflammatory language. Through the Community Independents movement, ordinary citizens have found an alternative way to participate in their democracy. A way that encourages respectful debate, finds common ground, and leads with values. This way may just safeguard Australian democracy from the perils of US politics, partisan fanaticism and becoming a society that has forgotten how to listen to one another.

1   Kelly (2024) "The balance is broken: What now for democracy", *The Australian*, p 80
2   Victorian Women's Trust (2021) "Kitchen Table Conversations: a guide for sustaining our democratic culture", https//www.vwt.org.au/projects/kitchen-table-conversations/

The Concrete Language of a Dying Planet

Anna Spargo-Ryan

In 2019, the *Guardian* published an article titled "'It's a crisis, not a change': the six *Guardian* language changes on climate matters". The language it had been using to describe environmental devastation did not accurately describe what was really happening. Editor-in-chief Katharine Viner said at the time, "We want to ensure that we are being scientifically precise, while also communicating clearly with readers …"

One of these changes replaced "biodiversity" with "wildlife". the *Guardian* called it "a bit less clinical". Actually, it is real.

Wildlife is part of the shared language we have to describe the most precarious and necessary parts of our world. A tiny displaced sugar glider. A beach lined with stranded pilot whales like dominos. The ruby trunk of a redwood tree being loaded onto a logging truck.

"Biodiversity" is abstract. It's a laboratory word, not a human one, too large to be tactile. By definition, it encompasses the variety of every living thing on Earth, from gnarled ancient forests to bacteria we leave in used tissues, making it a gift to climate denialists and greenwashers. A word so vast it can wildly overstate targets or play down impacts. Creating biodiversity is both leaving leftovers on the bench for a week and growing habitat for native fish species.

Abstract language is a terrible mechanism for communicating the specific nature and magnitude of any problem or its solution. In the case of climate change, that's to be expected: this terminology wasn't meant for the public; and scientists are not marketers.

Unfortunately, marketers *are* marketers. Within two decades of the coinage "global warming", spin doctors had got ahead of the science. The popularity of "climate change" itself was a deliberate political play in George W Bush's era — pollster Frank Luntz recommended it as a less scary alternative to "global warming", which itself already sounded more like cocktails with umbrellas than the widespread devastation of life as we know it.

But the reverse is also true: terms like "climate emergency" and "doomsday hellfire" are *so* scary that studies show they lead to disengagement and "active opposition to climate change policies".[1] The most well-meaning progressives are pushed to paralysis by fear tactics.

The problems with "biodiversity" and "climate change" spring from the same well: climate language is abstract, which pushes people away from action. And unless we fix it, our planet will burn.

Accessible, everyday words do communicate more clearly: concrete language triggers the parts of the brain used for mental navigation and spatial memory. It invokes more sensory interpretations: the lick of flame on an oily eucalypt is magnitudes more potent than a tree on fire.

But that's not all it does. Concreteness — that is, the opposite of abstractness — can have a measurable impact on a person's connection to the problem. Research from 2021 found that concrete imagery "significantly reduced perceived psychological distance to climate change".[2] While it doesn't necessarily move them to action, it does begin to break down our greatest challenge: indifference.

Despite campaigns that implicate consumers, greenhouse gas emissions are overwhelmingly the work of corporations. Since 2016, 80% of emissions have been produced by just 57 corporations.[3] According to the Carbon Majors Database Launch Report, most of these large producers — both privately and publicly owned — have *increased* fossil fuel output since the Paris Agreement.

This is the trick: co-opting scientific-sounding words that could mean anything. "Circularity" is a real term for getting the most out of resources and producing as little waste as possible, but in the hands of the environmental social governance team it becomes using only *mostly* virgin plastic. Sustainability reports — mandatory for Australian companies with more than $200 million in revenue — need only gesture at whoever's unlucky enough to be CEO 30 years from now, by which time we will all have been consumed by a megafire or floods, or both.

At the other end of the spectrum, progressive outlets increasingly evoke urgency with "climate crisis" or "climate catastrophe", which we know contributes to the same issue. Some insist on "human-driven climate change" to be absolutely clear about who has been burning fossil fuels since the Industrial Revolution while still using a fantastically broad term to describe the measurable impact of doing nothing.

The language of climate action has been co-opted and easily manipulated *because* it is non-specific: a mealy-mouthed policy for corporate compliance; vague handwringing to soothe share markets; heated strikes with no tangible demands; straight-up denial in pursuit of conservative votes.

For some, climate emergency is an unimaginable nightmare, fire raining from the sky onto the dried-out husk of the Earth. For others, global warming is the invention of a Swedish schoolgirl, clearly lying because it's snowing in March. We are rarely offered more clarity. We are dissuaded from finding a way forward because our imaginations are left to conjure exactly the images we need to remain stationary.

There is enormous power in embracing other ways of speaking about serious issues. Those with vested interests handed us the language of climate change and stopped us in our tracks. But no one controls the concrete words of a dying planet. We all do. And there is no time left to exclude anyone from this conversation.

1   Saab (2023) "Discourses of Fear on Climate Change in International Human Rights Law", *European Journal of International Law*, Vol 34, Issue 1, pp 113–135
2   Duan, Takahashi and Zwickle (2021) "The Moderating Role of Construal Level in Climate Change Visual Communication", *Science Communication*, 43(3), pp 358–387
3   https://carbonmajors.org

Worker Voice

Sally McManus

The Australian union movement has never been afraid of big ideas. Here's one: workers' voice should be embedded in decision-making everywhere.

Australia should abandon the American conflict-driven model of CEO supremacy enforced by top-down managerialism. Instead, we should embed workers' voice throughout decision-making and embrace the role of unions.

This idea is not new, but it is big given how dedicated employers and various governments have been to weakening and delegitimising the voice of working people. It is a simple principle, but it would be transformative. Working people should have a guaranteed voice in decisions that affect us.

This idea reflects a basic reality. It is the contribution that working people make that keeps Australia running. We are the teachers, the nurses, the stevedores, the public servants, the cleaners, the warehouse workers, the truck drivers, the community workers, the workers in every sector and industry upon whom this country and its future depends.

It is workers who will build Australia's future — using our skills, our expertise and our commitment. It should be commonsense in

Australia — as it is in many other places in the world — that workers and their unions should be active participants in the decisions that shape our lives. Decisions in the workplace, decisions in the economy, decisions in politics, and decisions in our communities. Respecting the voice of the people most integral to society means not just better decisions but it means everyone has a stake in the future.

However, our current system embeds conflict and exclusion. It is a system built for small ideas.

It is the reality of the current system that workers have to fight tooth and nail for basic pay increases that just keep up with CPI, let alone to get a fair share of productivity gains their work has created. In many circumstances, employers can impose change without negotiating with their workers. This is self-defeating. Not only does it diminish working people's rights, it means employers do not get the benefit of the input of their workforce; as a result the accumulated knowledge, experience and skill that workers could bring to this process is ignored.

Working people often have just one chance every three years to exercise their right to negotiate with the option of "protected" industrial action. Most employers do not make big changes during this window and workers are forced to fight rearguard actions and to approach bargaining as their one chance to get any improvements in working conditions. This is not a recipe for cooperation. It creates conflict and distrust.

Look at where this path has taken the US. Large sections of the population there are giving up on democracy, especially the working class. Decisions are made about them by billionaires and men in suits whether they are in corporate offices, on Wall Street, or in the White House. Many feel abandoned and angry as wealth continues to be taken from them and is more and more centralised in the hands of a few.

In our country there is also deep cynicism in working-class communities. Workers in outer suburbs spend time stuck in traffic and working their guts out in multiple jobs. People in regional areas watch housing become just as unaffordable as the cities, and all the while everyone sees the profits of the big companies of Australia grow and grow. These same companies price gouge while ordinary people struggle.

The positive is that we have bought ourselves more time as the industrial relations changes made by the Albanese government will help workers claw back pay rises, address gender inequity and job insecurity. The government's Future Made in Australia package plans to bring back manufacturing, to look after communities affected by the energy transition, as well as creating the next generations of jobs. This will also make a big difference.

But the problem is, these changes can all be taken away by a future government. In fact, Peter Dutton is already promising to do just that. People like Dutton and Gina Rinehart may well welcome a more authoritarian, less democratic country full of division and cynicism.

So, change has to be more profound and much deeper. If we really want to transform our country for the better, worker voice should be embedded in decision-making structures so that we move away from the culture of conflict we have had since colonisation. This will require employers recognising there is a better way to approach negotiation, one that begins with treating their workers with respect.

This change in culture will also benefit businesses. If working people's skills, experience and knowledge are genuinely incorporated into processes of decision-making, and workers have a stake in these decisions, it could unleash benefits to enterprises that simply cannot be achieved in the context of a race-to-the-bottom culture of short-termism.

Respecting and engaging the workforce means respecting and engaging those they elect to represent them. Employers should abandon their opposition to unionism. They should recognise the benefits of having a representative voice of their workforces to engage and negotiate with. As a country we need to move away from negotiations being a simple slugfest over wages and make consultation a normal way of doing business. This means involving workers at every step along the way.

Governments should ensure working people have a voice on every issue that affects them. The CEO and Board Club of Australia should be opened up to worker representatives. Governments at every level should ensure workers' voices are included in decision-making. Both money and power need to be redistributed.

There are already examples of where concepts such as tripartism work well and have delivered. These are some of the most economically productive countries in the world — and also the happiest. Nordic countries have enjoyed both economic success and continued improvements in quality of life across the population. There is a reason these countries consistently rank at the top of the world happiness index. As Associate Professor Chris F Wright from the University of Sydney has explained, these countries embedded workers' voice through unions in their bargaining and economic systems, enabling "workers to engage with employers on equal terms". This has created mechanisms that "give workers voice and empower them to identify productive work practices, which is good for business".

I am not suggesting that we seek to directly replicate these models — but we do need to learn the big lessons from them: we can do so much better. Respect for workers' voice will deliver improvements in both economic performance and quality of life for all Australians.

How to Plan Cities for Climate Change

Lucy Hughes Turnbull AO

The certainty and imminence of climate change has been with us for at least four decades. Our preparation for it in the field of urban planning and city building has been slow and we are not there yet. We need to make changes now to make our cities more resilient to the effect of extreme climate events.

Terms like "heat dome" and "rain bomb" are recent. I had never heard of "heat bulb temperature" or "lethal humidity" before last year. Whenever new things start happening, new words and phrases emerge — think "telephone", "computer", "internet", "smartphone". And we are learning a new vocabulary to describe the effects of climate change all the time.

The planet is heating, apparently faster and more than we hoped it would. So, we must adapt and design our houses, our neighbourhoods, towns and cities to make life as safe and as bearable as possible in extreme events.

Climate change is with us, breathing down our neck, killing people in heatwaves, drowning us in rainstorms, and making us less safe. Those who are already the most socio-economically or physically vulnerable are also the most vulnerable to extreme events, mostly through reduced ability to "hang the expense" on hot days and to use one of the best inventions of the 20th century — air conditioning. And disadvantaged people are often under the most housing stress, least able to afford to retrofit their housing for greater insulation.

We do not have time to waste.

Extreme heat

Extreme heat can kill people silently, mostly in their home. So, there is no dramatic video footage to project onto screens as there is with storms, cyclones and floods. Heatwaves do get dramatic and televisual when roads, railways and bridges buckle and warp and we are stuck in public transport when the electricity supply stops, and when there are mass casualty events, as there was during the 2024 Hajj pilgrimage in Saudi Arabia.

Well-connected neighbourhoods, both spatially and socially, can support those who are vulnerable to extreme heat. And everyone else. Neighbourhoods that are walkable and less motor-vehicle dependent are more likely to achieve this as more day-to-day contact means people can check on each other informally.

At a community level, in extreme heatwaves, vulnerable people need ready access to cooling centres. For the middle class, we call this a shopping mall, or our offices, or air-conditioned homes. But for vulnerable people, community facilities like libraries and other indoor public places need to be called into action as formally designated places for people to cool down.

These cooling centres are already widely advertised in the US at a local level during extreme events. Some of these places are located close to public housing in metropolitan centres. We need to start designating cooling centres at a local level here in Australia. Each local government has or should have the capacity to do this.

At a household level, we need to live in energy efficient homes. Typical suburban dwellings in Australia are not designed for thermal efficiency during heatwaves. The millions of dark tiled roofs, the predominance of hard surfaces and lack of tree canopy and overhanging eaves to shield homes from the sun in many suburban homes is testament to that. Many houses act as hotboxes more than as shelters from oppressive heat.

We have not followed the ancient wisdom of Vitruvius to design a house for its site, latitude and climate. Our ancestors did it much better before air conditioning because there was no alternative! With technology we have imagined we can ignore design and the need for shade and canopy in hot weather. Even the "humble" terrace house did a better job with its covered first-floor balconies, thick walls, French doors and reasonable cross ventilation. The mid-20th century brick and masonry apartments built along train lines of our larger Australian cities — not so very different from the Roman "insulae" or medium-density apartments that lined the streets of Roman cities — are better than many contemporary developments. Medium density reduces most dwellings' exposure to the sun and therefore heat.

Medium-density housing was an intelligent response that existed for millennia, making it possible to walk to shops, services and public transport. And a chance to be connected with each other as we walk around. Until the advent of suburbs designed for the motor car after 1950, these four-, six- or eight-pack medium-density or "gentle density" apartments were the basic building blocks of neighbourhoods and communities.

We need to relearn the wisdom of the ancients and unlearn the mistakes of the 20th century when we thought we could tame the world in general, nature in particular, and the temperature in our homes through new-fangled devices like air conditioning. The ubiquitous use of the motor vehicle made more compact housing and walkability less necessary.

Extreme rain events and rain bombs

Events like the Lismore floods are likely to become more common. There have been many one-in-a-hundred-year events there, and other parts of Australia in the last 20 years. That tells us there is something troubling about the accuracy of flood modelling.

As a society, we need to be confident in the accuracy of planning and land-use zoning. There is some concern it is not being updated enough. Melbourne Water released its first metropolitan flood modelling map in twenty years recently.

Extreme heat is not an event that can be insured against. But flooding is. At least, up to now and for as long as the insurance market remains viable. Extreme rain events and other climate risks like bushfires could make some areas uninsurable, which would lead to a sudden decline in homeowners' land values.

Information about flood vulnerability really matters. Insurers probably know more about an area's flood vulnerability than any government agency because they are seeing the flow of claims and they have a direct economic interest in pricing insurance, as do organisations like ClimateValuation.com, a part of the Climate Risk Group. So, if organisations like Melbourne Water and ClimateValuation.com are declaring areas or suburbs vulnerable to flooding, to the point of being uninsurable, we must take notice and, more importantly, action. We can only ever be resilient if we are conscious of risk and act upon it.

In NSW, for the most part, flood mapping is the task of local governments. I would argue this is not the right level of government to do this and the principle of subsidiarity should not apply. Local governments have less access to information about flow-on effects from wider level river and drainage systems upstream which are not within the LGA; this is the case especially where local government is small in comparison to the size of the river and drainage systems. There are inefficiencies and duplications in multiple local governments looking at flooding risk. This is not just a question of whether the one-in-a-hundred-year flood maps are accurate — flood maps for more frequent and the "probable maximum flood" information should also be available and readily accessible for homeowners and buyers. We know insurers seek this information out. It is only fair that homeowners and buyers have it too.

The way forward

The good news is that access to green space is not only what people want, it is also a practical way to mitigate urban heat and to make areas spongier and more able to absorb water from heavy rains. Those sorts of green improvements can happen at a micro, neighbourhood level, especially with greenfield development and by taking advantage of under-utilised golf courses.

In general, if we reduce the proportion of hard concrete surfaces (which are a major cause of the urban heat-island effect), and turn down the heat and pressure on stressed urban systems with new green spaces, which can be as small as a tennis court, we could reduce heat and improve biodiversity and quality of life.
We need to fight for change at the community level so that the designs of our houses, buildings and streetscapes help foster resilience and build a more comfortable future.

The Right Kind of Action: Tackling the Housing Crisis

Maiy Azize

Australia is in the midst of a historic housing crisis. "Crisis" is a politically charged word, but with record-high-housing costs, renters living with no security, and more and more people in housing stress, it is the only way to describe the experiences of countless Australians on the frontlines of a massive policy failure.

The agencies working on the crisis have been sounding the alarm for years. There are stories about pensioners competing for rooms in sharehouses, people in full-time work on the brink of homelessness, and families living in tents and cars. Many of the workers trying to support these people are themselves struggling to keep a roof over their heads.

These stories are borne out by statistics. Research from the Everybody's Home national campaign has found that essential workers can't afford average rents anywhere in the country[1], that housing costs are trapping women in dangerous relationships[2], and that the housing crisis is worsening anxiety and mental health for many Australians.[3]

After each grim report, commentators ask when we will see real action. The truth is that there has been action. The wrong kind.

The past four decades have marked a major shift in how the federal government approaches housing. For years before that, the government's solution to housing affordability was a simple one. It built, rented and sold homes. Australians from all walks of life rented and bought these homes, from teachers and public servants to construction and manufacturing workers. At its peak, almost one in four new homes was being built by the government[4] and as recently as the early 80s, one in three renters was renting from the government.[5] This provided secure homes for people who needed them, and it kept housing costs down for everyone.

This approach changed in the 80s and 90s when the government began relying on the private market to supply and distribute homes. Instead of providing affordable homes, it began offering rent-assistance payments to people in the private market, grants to first-home buyers, and tax handouts for property investors. Commonwealth Rent Assistance was introduced in the 80s for renters in the private market and has become the federal government's largest housing assistance program.[6] Negative gearing deductions were formalised in 1987, allowing investors to write off their losses at the expense of the taxpayer. In 1999, the Howard Government introduced the capital gains tax discount, allowing more investors to make windfall profits from property sales.

In the years that have followed, private supply and investor incentives have continued to be the solution the developer lobby and many politicians favour. Australia now builds anywhere between 165,000 and 240,000 new homes each year[7], growing faster than our population. We have never had more homes per person[8], yet the homes we have are more unfairly distributed than they've ever been.

It is governments' decisions to put housing supply in the hands of for-profit developers, coupled with a tax system that privileges the already wealthy, that has fuelled our housing crisis — and this system hasn't come cheap. Lining the pockets of private, for-profit housing interests costs the federal Budget around $80 billion each year.[9] That is orders of magnitude more than the government spends on delivering homes itself. The federal government spends just $1.8 billion each year on social housing.[10] The number of new homes the public or community sectors builds is a fraction of what it was in the 50s, and the idea that the government could ever step up and provide homes to ordinary Australians again is either ignored or mocked by our major political parties.

Many people believe that our housing system is broken and that the solutions are complex and difficult to identify. That view is well-meaning, but it is wrong. The brutal reality is that Australia's housing system is working exactly the way it was designed to work, pumping billions of dollars into the private market and hurting average Australians in the process. It is the result of government decisions and government spending — the wrong kind.

Turning this crisis around is only possible if the federal government flips this formula on its head and takes back control of housing. The first thing it needs to do is phase out investor handouts that are making inequality worse and pushing up the cost of housing. Abolishing the capital gains tax discount and negative gearing will mean that taxpayers stop lining the pockets of investors to outbid ordinary buyers. The landlords who sell in response to a change like this are the ones most likely to be making a loss that is underwritten by the taxpayer — and the ones most likely to be driving large rent increases.

The second thing the government needs to do is get back to delivering homes itself. Australia has a massive social-housing shortfall, with 640,000 homes needed to fill the gap.[11] If the government is serious about bringing costs down, it would go even further than this and aim for 15% of all homes to be social housing. This would mean that social housing is not just a safety net for the few, but a real option for more Australians.

There is simply no way to bring costs down and guarantee a home for every Australian unless the government steps up and takes the same kind of responsibility it shows in critical areas like health and education. There are no comparable countries that have turned around their housing crises, or avoided them altogether, without the government playing a major role.

Tackling this crisis will take time and a willingness to put the interests of Australians who need a home ahead of developers, investors and naysayers who won't accept that the current approach is failing. But with the crisis worsening every year, the stakes couldn't be higher. It's time for the federal government to step up and take the right kind of action on housing.

1   Everybody's Home (2023), "Priced Out: An Index of Affordable Rentals for Australia's Essential Workers"
2   Everybody's Home and Equity Economics (2021) "Nowhere to Go: The benefits of providing long-term social housing to women that have experienced domestic and family violence"
3   Everybody's Home (2023), "Brutal Reality: The Human Cost of Australia's Housing Crisis"
4   Australian Bureau of Statistics (2023) *Building Activity, Australia*, Table 38
5   Everybody's Home (2024), "Written Off: The high cost of Australia's unfair tax system"
6   See Budget Paper 2, Budget 2024–25
7   Australian Bureau of Statistics (2023), *Building Activity, Australia*, Table 38
8   See the Census of Population and Housing
9   Everybody's Home (2024) "Written Off: The high cost of Australia's unfair tax system"
10 See the National Agreement on Social Housing and Homelessness
11 UNSW City Futures Centre (2022), "Quantifying Australia's unmet housing need: A national snapshot"

Proportional Representation: The Key to Restoring Democracy

Christine Milne AO

Australia is on the verge of a paradigm shift. The bold assumption of the past 50 years that the free market is the solution to everything has been tested and discredited. Neoliberal economics, social policy and politics implemented by both Labor and Liberal National governments since the mid-1970s have transformed our country, but not in the way that people were promised.

Although they might not be able to name "small government, privatisation, deregulation", the hallmarks of neoliberal ideology, as being responsible, people know business as usual is failing them.

Instead of solutions, at the global and national level, we now face problems so overwhelming that they threaten our very survival. We face the interconnected existential crises of global heating, biodiversity collapse and deepening inequality. We are seeing a rapidly deteriorating natural environment, inadequate health and education services and our democratic system of government transformed into a plutocracy delivering for big business. State and federal governments, Labor and the LNP are different only by degree, not by direction.

Does anyone doubt that Labor WA, for example, now stands for Woodside's Agenda?

People have had enough and are demanding change in what governments do and how they do it. Delivering that change requires voters regaining confidence in our democratic system of government. The only way that will happen is by taking it back from the plutocrats and making the public interest the highest priority in government and in institutions like the public service. It will be the political fight of our lives, and it has already begun.

Voting patterns show people will not take "No" for an answer. Since 2000, the combined vote for the so-called "parties of government", the Labor, Liberal and National parties, has declined to the point where less than 70% of people vote for any of them. Every opinion poll and community meeting shows people want governments to intervene in the public interest. They want funding for public schools and public hospitals. They want to be represented in Parliament by people who are listening to them and delivering for them and not for the corporate lobbyists. They want the diverse representation offered by small parties and independents.

The stage is set for the two major battlefields of debate of big ideas for the next 20 years: what policy change will deliver the solutions people want and how can that change be delivered?

"What polices will deliver change" will be *vigorously* contested by academics, policy analysts, think tanks, NGOs and media moguls. But it will not be too different in substance or philosophical alignment from the policy debates to which we are accustomed. "How to deliver that change" will be *viciously* contested.

The big idea whose time has come, the big idea for "how" to deliver change, is electoral reform. Adopting proportional representation in all houses of government, state and federal, is the fundamental step.

Corporations rely on the traditional "parties of government" in Australia, Labor or the LNP, to take donations from them and deliver for them. Failure to do so results in electoral loss. Our democracy is now run by a handful of companies from which key people are selected to run government institutions, develop government policy and consult on how to implement it. Corporations determine the parameters of policy which both "parties of government" take to elections and the guard rails inside which the degree of any reform is debated.

We must move to shared power so that our parliamentarians represent us in the proportions for which we voted for them. We need to move beyond the corporate-owned and controlled two-party system in which the only "parties of government" accepted by them are Labor or a coalition between the Liberal and National parties.

To deliver transformative change, as opposed to incremental or temporary change, we need to overturn the idea that Labor and the LNP are the only acceptable parties of government whether majority or minority.

It is true that minority government can and does drive and deliver change especially if government is delivered as a result of policy negotiation. But if a minority government reneges on its agreements, what then?

The lesson of history is that what is not secured before a government is sworn in will not be achieved and even when agreed, is by no means assured. The failure of the minority Gillard government to deliver on its agreement with the Greens to address political donations is a case in point. The only reason it legislated a carbon price, the Clean Energy Package by 1 July 2012, is because the Greens made it a condition of supporting Labor. No price, no timeframe, no Gillard government.

The package had integrity and brought down emissions because the Greens insisted on the formation of a Multi-Party Climate Committee informed by experts and insisted on additional measures like a $10 billion fund off budget to incentivise the transition to renewable energy. The Greens would not have passed it if the government had given in to corporate interests to enable 100% offsets and increasing concessions to energy intensive industries as they had done with the CPRS.

Ironically, because Labor wouldn't agree to raise its target of 5% emissions reduction below 2000 levels by 2020, the emissions trading scheme had to operate with a fixed price which was higher than the ETS would have delivered. It was not a tax, but it had the same effect as a carbon tax. Australia had shown that pricing carbon worked.

Emissions trading is a corporate initiative, a market mechanism that can only be effective with a target and timeframe appropriate to the scale and urgency of the global heating crisis. That will never happen in our corporate-controlled parliaments. Its time has passed. We are in an emergency and direct government intervention through taxation, incentives and regulation is the quickest, cheapest and most effective way forward. Just as fires and floods demand emergency intervention, so too does global heating.

But such intervention in a free market is intolerable to neoliberalist corporate Australia and to Labor and the LNP. With the passage of the Clean Energy Package in 2012, corporate Australia understood that momentarily it had lost control of the Parliament and the neoliberal agenda. It made sure it regained it with the election of Tony Abbott as prime minister at the 2013 election, and it hasn't relinquished it since.

That is why the way to effect change is to change the system. We have to lift our level of ambition. We have to dump the idea that minority government by a "party of government" backed by independents and small parties is sufficient to drive long-lasting change and take back our democracy. It isn't.

A greater number of independents and small parties elected is not enough to overturn corporate control. Even with Labor or Coalition minority governments, they will always vote together to defeat their small party or crossbench supporters to oppose, weaken or reduce ambition in legislation. Once in government, the community and those members of Parliament who put them there are ditched if the corporate donors to Labor and the LNP are threatened in any significant way. Approving new coal mines, gas fields, supporting ongoing native-forest logging or encouraging gambling are cases in point.

Federal minority governments hold all ministries and, with the exception of a limited number of policies agreed by those who have delivered the numbers for government, control the budget, the policy agenda, the recommendations of all parliamentary inquiries and key appointments to regulatory bodies.

The Albanese Labor government and its corporate donors secured a majority in the House of Representatives with a primary vote of 32.58% and a minority in the Senate. Yet, with less than a third of votes, it holds all ministries and has been able to defeat the ambitions of those serious about climate by not legislating beyond the 43% and the Safeguard Mechanism that the fossil fuel industry will tolerate.

It is time for negotiated agreements between all parties and independents — not just "parties of government" — to form multi-party governments that share power and policy, budgets, ministries and the day-to-day operations of government. It occurs in European democracies and in New Zealand; there is no reason it cannot happen here.

Proportional representation doesn't need a referendum, it needs political will. It needs people to stand up and campaign for the restoration of democracy. The policy vacuum created by the end of neoliberalism creates that opportunity.

As Nelson Mandela said, "Everything is impossible until it is done."

Truth, Transparency and Whistleblowing: The Case for a Federal Whistleblower Protection Authority

Kieran Pender

A series of major scandals. High-profile cases of whistleblowers being mistreated. Rising calls for stronger protections for those who act in the public interest to courageously expose wrongdoing. An emphasis on the importance of truth and transparency.

This is a fair summary of the state of transparency and integrity in Australia's democracy in 2024. In recent years, whistleblowers have been essential in ensuring accountability for wrongdoing that has rocked the nation. Robodebt, war crimes in Afghanistan, environmental degradation, corruption, human rights abuses in the aged-care and disability sectors, price gouging by supermarkets — the list goes on. Praise for whistleblowers, and calls for stronger protections, have been a consistent theme in newspaper front pages, royal commissions and parliamentary inquiries.

Yet despite the growing recognition of the democratic importance of whistleblowing, Australia's truth-tellers continue to suffer. In the past decade, four high-profile whistleblowers have been prosecuted. Witness K was given a suspended sentence for exposing Australia's wrongdoing against Timor-Leste; his lawyer Bernard Collaery was dragged through a secret prosecution process until the Albanese government dropped the matter. In May 2024, David McBride was sentenced to almost six years in prison for leaking documents to the national broadcaster, which formed the basis for the landmark Afghan Files reporting. The following month, Richard Boyle — who exposed unethical conduct at the Australian Taxation Office — lost an appeal against a ruling that found he is not protected from prosecution by whistleblowing laws.

These high-profile cases are the tip of the iceberg. As many as eight in ten whistleblowers face some form of workplace retaliation for speaking up. Australia's whistleblower protection framework, particularly for the federal public service, is complex and inaccessible, with too many loopholes and too few robust protections. Promised reform has yet to materialise. Whistleblowers are staying silent; wrongdoing is going unchecked. And all of us suffer as a result.

But the scandals, the plight of whistleblowers and the calls for stronger protections are also reminiscent of 1994. Thirty years ago, in the same year The Australia Institute was formed, the first federal parliamentary inquiry into whistleblower protections reported. The Fitzgerald Inquiry led to the first-ever whistleblowing law in Queensland. Subsequent corporate and government sagas across the nation, which featured whistleblower mistreatment, prompted the formation of the Senate Select Committee on Public Interest Whistleblowing. One of its key recommendations remains salient three decades on: the need for a federal whistleblower protection authority. The report is a reminder that good ideas are timeless.

Thirty years later, the need for a whistleblower protection authority is more compelling than ever. In 2017, in the wake of the financial sector scandals that led to the banking royal commission, a bipartisan joint parliamentary committee recommended that "a one-stop shop Whistleblower Protection Authority be established to cover both the public and private sectors".

Ahead of the 2019 election, Labor committed to the idea — in a press release, then-shadow Attorney-General Mark Dreyfus KC said he would "strengthen protections for whistleblowers through the establishment of a Whistleblower Protection Authority, a one-stop shop to support and protect whistleblowers".

Regrettably, that good idea is as yet unrealised. Crossbench proposals to include a whistleblowing authority within a federal anti-corruption body did not form part of Labor's bill to establish the National Anti-Corruption Commission.

Despite progress at state level — including beefed-up whistleblower protection functions within the New South Wales Ombudsman following reform in 2022, and similar recommendations from a 2023 review into whistleblowing in Queensland — the federal government's position remains at the stage of considering the need for such a body (that consideration is ongoing at the time of writing, and limited to the public sector whistleblowing framework). Despite the proliferation of similar bodies internationally — there is a longstanding whistleblower protection authority for American public servants, and more recent authorities are already having an impact in the Netherlands and Slovakia — the Albanese government is yet to heed the clarion call of successive reports and inquiries.

What, exactly, would such a body do? The 1994 report describes a good starting point, although of course our collective understanding of the whistleblowing landscape is significantly more advanced three decades on. That is why, in February, the Human Rights Law

Centre, Transparency International Australia and Griffith University jointly published draft design principles for a whistleblower protection authority. Developed with the input of civil society partners, ex-whistleblowers, corporate experts and former senior public servants, the principles set out the framework for an effective, enduring body. The principles were also informed by the international experience, borrowing the best of what has worked in other jurisdictions.

On our principles, the body would be able to receive whistleblowers and refer them to investigative agencies as appropriate, retaining some oversight function of those investigations and the treatment of whistleblowers. Critically, the authority would be able to receive complaints when whistleblowers are mistreated, investigate the complaints and take remedial action as appropriate. It would also provide a case-worker-style support function, guiding whistleblowers through what is often a taxing process. It could bring strategic enforcement action, much like the Fair Work Ombudsman, and offer alternative dispute resolution, just like the Australian Human Rights Commission. The authority would also administer schemes for whistleblowers to access external support, including from lawyers and psychologists, and have education, training and advocacy functions. Truly "a one-stop shop to support and protect whistleblowers".

Establishing an independent and appropriately resourced whistleblower protection authority is not a panacea. But it will represent a step forward for truth-telling in this country. Together with comprehensive reform to public and private sector whistleblower protection laws, and ongoing cultural change, a whistleblowing authority can turn on the light after a decade of darkness. Such a body can become an essential part of Australia's integrity landscape, and enhance the effectiveness of existing regulatory agencies.

Recent years have not been kind to truth and transparency in Australia: the 2019 press raids; the whistleblower prosecutions, including the imprisonment of McBride and the ongoing case against Boyle; a lack of comprehensive reform. But if it is darkest before the dawn, perhaps we are on the cusp of the establishment of a whistleblower protection authority that would herald a new era for openness and accountability in Australian public life. This is a big idea — and its time has come.

No Backbone

Dr Richard Denniss

Economies don't have "backbones", exports aren't "good for the economy" and the fossil fuel industry contributes a tiny percentage of government revenue and jobs in Australia. All of these claims are easy to check, but facts don't fare well in modern Australian debate.

But let's pretend, just for a minute, that economies do have a skeleton running through the middle of them and that exports provided the solid framework on which all other parts of the economy were based. If that were the case then in Victoria the backbone would be education, in Tasmania it would be tourism and in South Australia it would be food and wine. According to Australia's trade data the Australian economy is clearly not just a quarry.

But let's keep pretending, just for another minute. If exports were so important to our economy, and governments would never do anything to harm our export industries, then why would the Albanese government even contemplate putting a cap on educational exports from our publicly owned universities? If exports were so important, why wouldn't governments be encouraging more education exports, not less?

Now, stick with me here. I can think of a number of reasons why the government might want to put a cap on all sorts of exports, including higher education. Indeed, contrary to the narrative that exports are vitally important, a narrative fossil fuel industry boosters love to perpetuate, governments limit all sorts of exports all the time. It's just in Australia we aren't allowed to talk about when or why as, if we did, people might ask why we export so much of the coal and gas that, when burned, is causing dangerous climate change.

There is no such thing as "free trade". If there were, it wouldn't take 271 pages to draft a free trade agreement between Australia and the US. Indeed it's only because both the US and Australian governments are so opposed to free trade that it takes so many pages to spell out all the restrictions on exports and imports that both countries agree are a good idea. The political power of the sugar industry in the US ensured the US is implacably opposed to Australia's ability to freely trade in sugar. Likewise the political hostility to machine-gun ownership in Australia ensures that our government insists on restrictions on the export of US assault rifles to Australia. Both countries have bans on exports and imports of heroin, cocaine and methamphetamines even though all those substances are widely consumed in both countries. Limiting the movement of goods over borders is simply what governments do.

Now that we know that politics always trumps the idea of free trade we can take a closer, and more honest, look at how often Australia restricts its exports. Iron ore exports from Australia were banned in 1936 due, in part, to fears of Japanese military expansion in the Pacific. That said, despite Japan's defeat in 1945 it was not until 1960 that the Menzies government began to partially remove restrictions on iron ore exports, restrictions that were not fully lifted until 1966.

Perhaps the most famous cap on exports in Australia was Labor's so-called "three mines" policy for uranium, which was introduced under Bob Hawke in 1984 and lasted until John Howard repealed it in 1996. Significantly, Labor's ban on uranium export expansion did not prevent other counties from buying or selling uranium, and nor did it end nuclear proliferation around the world. It was, however, seen to be the right thing to do. Labor's moratorium on new uranium mines held until 2007 when Kevin Rudd led the charge for its removal, a decision Anthony Albanese opposed at the time, publicly at least. Queensland, Victoria and New South Wales all still have bans on uranium mines in place even though their construction would lead to an increase in exports. Bizarrely, Chris Bowen publicly says that calls for no new gas and coal mines are "a slogan not a policy", but in reality, bans on dangerous things is one of the oldest and most effective policies of all, one Labor has long embraced.

Morality, as opposed to export maximisation, played a major role in Australia's imposition of a wide range on sanctions on South Africa. While Gough Whitlam and Malcolm Fraser showed leadership in their support for sporting and cultural sanctions, it was the Hawke Labor government's willingness to build global support for financial sanctions against the Apartheid regime that made a big impact. In the words of former Labor Foreign Minister Gareth Evans, "Why did successive Australian governments commit so much effort to resolving a situation so little of our making? I think the short answer lies in that instinct for good international citizenship that, despite periodic lapses by various governments (and oppositions) that ought to know better, is part of our national psyche."

If Australian government policy was designed to maximise our exports then we would still be exporting whale meat, asbestos and platypus skins around the world. If exports were our number one goal then why do we limit the export of weapons, widely used recreational drugs or human organs? To be clear, Australia never has, and never will be, an export maximiser. No country is.

Of course our political class know all this, which is why there is bipartisan support for curtailing the ability of Australia's higher education sector to export educational services. Indeed, in the words of Liberal Senator Andrew Bragg "the Australian Dream is more important than any export industry".

I agree.

The fossil fuel industry has successfully conflated the idea of export revenue with government revenue when the concepts are entirely unrelated. Many believe, wrongly, that gas exports pay for our schools and hospitals, when in reality we give more than half the gas we export away for free.

When Australian governments choose to give our gas away royalty-free to foreign-owned companies like Chevron or Inpex, and choose to legislate a Petroleum Resource Rent Tax that has, literally, never collected a cent from foreign-owned gas export projects such as Shell's Prelude LNG terminal, then while the billions of dollars worth of exports are "counted" in Australia's GDP, none of those export dollars flow into the coffers of our state or federal budgets. None. Foreign-owned companies getting gas for free and paying no tax here in Australia aren't propping up our economy, they are freeloading.

In Norway they heavily tax their fossil fuel industry and give their kids free university education. In Australia we heavily subsidise our fossil fuel industry and charge our kids a fortune to go to university. The Australian Government collects more money from HECS than it gets from our Petroleum Resource Rent Tax. Government choices matter.

Economies don't have backbones. No healthy economy is built on any one industry, but they are always built on strong communities, great infrastructure and thriving democracies. Luckily for Australia, more than 99% of Australians don't work in fossil fuel production and the GST alone contributes far more revenue to our state and federal budgets than the entire fossil fuel industry.

Andrew Bragg is right, no export industry is more important than the Australian dream and Anthony Albanese is right that it's okay to curtail any export industry if you believe it's in the national interest. Chris Bowen might claim banning new gas and coal mines is a "slogan not a policy" but according to both opinion polling and climate science it's actually very good at being both. And according to former Labor Foreign Minister Gareth Evans, doing the right thing for the world as a whole used to be what Australian governments did. Maybe a future government will think like that again one day, hopefully not before it is too late.

The Mental Health Crisis and Solutions

Professor Patrick McGorry AO

The landscape of mental health

In the post-COVID era, after two decades of relentless awareness raising, Australians are more conscious than ever that our mental health is fragile, hostage to not only our innate vulnerabilities, but equally to the ebbs and flows of fortune, and to powerful megatrends that seem out of our control.

Particularly since the middle of the last century when infectious disease receded in the developed world through vaccines and antimicrobial treatments, mental illness has been one of the leading causes of health burden, and the non-communicable disease that causes the most damage to economic growth and productivity. However, there is now unequivocal evidence that the prevalence of mental ill health has been steadily increasing in many high- and middle-income nations that reliably measure these trends, and in low-income countries too. This increase is dramatic and yet largely confined to adolescents and emerging adults. Their precarious developmental stage is characterised by the greatest vulnerability for onset of adult forms of mental illness, with 75% of mental disorders emerging before the age of 25.

In Australia we have seen the prevalence of mental ill health at the full diagnostic threshold, indicating a need for care, rising from 26% in 2007 to 39% in 2021. This is an alarming 50% jump in need for care, even more serious in women. Similar trends have been observed in the US, the UK and a number of other nations. The US Surgeon General, Dr Vivek Murthy, warned the President in 2022 that the nation was facing a "youth mental health crisis", and has been actively campaigning for serious responses ever since. The Household, Income and Labour Dynamics in Australia survey contains a robust mental-health measure that tracks the crisis back to the early 2000s, revealing that millennials and Gen Z are principally affected, and that the pandemic had an additionally potent cohort effect that has persisted, which spawned the term "shadow pandemic".

Some have speculated that greater awareness and help-seeking, combined with an expansion of the boundaries for the diagnosis of common mental disorders, such as anxiety and depression, has triggered a form of sociogenic "contagion", which has also driven the surge in diagnosis-seeking behaviour associated with autism spectrum disorders (ASD) and Attention Deficit Hyperactivity Disorder (ADHD). While these forces are real, they do not go close to accounting for the rise in genuine illness, which requires expert mental health care. The methodology of the ABS National Mental Health Survey involves rigorous community sampling methods independent of help-seeking and self-reported distress, is interview based and ensures that the diagnosis prevalence estimates are sound, and do not merely reflect "distress". Sceptics must not be allowed to gaslight the very substantial number of Australians with a genuine and urgent need for health care.

Despite this growing public health crisis, mental health care in Australia has not only remained the poor cousin within the health system, but has actually deteriorated in terms of access and quality over recent years, despite the false perception that there has been greater investment. Spending on mental health care as a proportion of the health budget has fallen to a new low of 6.8%, despite the health burden due to mental illness sitting between 15 and 20%. Mental health expenditure has merely risen with inflation. This neglect is mirrored across the globe.

Mental health research receives an equally raw deal from Australian medical research and philanthropic funders, notably the National Health and Medical Research Council and the Medical Research Future Fund, with funding at 7% or less of the total scheme. This is despite the fact that the quality and impact of Australian mental health research is benchmarked at third or fourth in the world and outperforms more celebrated areas such as cancer and cardiovascular research.

On the ground, following the closure of the 19th century asylums in the 1990s, downsized state-government-funded services now operated through large acute hospital networks have not only failed to grow in the face of increased need but have been eroded, and then more or less collapsed under the pressure. The culture and standard of care has become quite debased with poor morale and disempowered leadership; services have devolved to a counter-therapeutic culture of risk management, and despite genuine research advances, are now less evidence-based than ever. It is a traumatic and dispiriting world of pain for staff and patients alike, despite the best efforts of those clinicians who soldier on and resist the exodus into the more protected and affluent, yet fragmented and often lonely, cocoon of private practice.

The cumulative neglect across the system eventually culminated in a royal commission in Victoria after the then Premier Daniel Andrews, with admirable honesty, admitted that the system was "broken". Despite a mental-health levy, little has changed. Other states are no different. Federally there have been some world-leading innovations at the primary-care level for both young people and adults, but they are modest and are now eroding too. Furthermore, the "missing middle" of more complex illness, which involves a staggering 1 to 2 million Australians, simply cannot access mental health care of appropriate quality and duration in a timely and engaging way.

Megatrends

Richard Eckersley pointed out many years ago that young people are the miners' canaries of society. While mental illness was already a major but grossly neglected source of disease burden, it is to the powerful socio-economic megatrends that we must look to understand why mental health is deteriorating so alarmingly. There is a range of candidates, such as climate change, social media, economic stress and intergenerational inequality. There are some strong temporal associations, especially the rise of social media and smartphones, which some analysts, such as Jonathan Haidt and Jean Twenge, believe are the overwhelming driver of the youth mental-health crisis. However we should remember that for every complex problem there is a simple solution, which is wrong. Moral panic has surfaced in relation to every new technological advance, from novels to television. Social media has very harmful effects alongside some benefits; however, the youth mental-health crisis has a number of contributory causes, not one. It will be challenging to design methodologies to accurately allocate the attributable causal fraction to the various candidate causes, so opinion and mere plausibility are likely to rule unless we are cautious.

Solutions

Whenever a surge in prevalence of this magnitude occurs in a health domain, whether rapidly, when we use the term epidemic, or more gradually, the need for prevention comes much more clearly into focus. Prevention is feasible to an extent for most mental disorders, but all of the new candidate megatrends, and especially if they are driven by the invisible engine of neoliberal ideology, will be extremely difficult to counter, even if there were an ideological global shift. This is why the initial response from Haidt and many politicians has been to focus on what seems doable, such as restricting the access of young people to smartphones and the internet until a particular age. Even this may be difficult, and it risks letting off the real culprits, the private technofeudalists who fail to ensure that the social media platforms of Tik Tok, X, Meta and Instagram are safe spaces. Restrictions forced selectively upon young people will have unforeseen negative impacts, and any remedial measures need to be considered in consultation with them.

So, in the meantime, the immediate response must involve a reimagining of Australia's innovative and formerly world-leading system of youth mental health care. Subsequently we need mental health reform that embraces the whole of the lifespan. Headspace, the youth mental health foundation, is in urgent need of redesign, reinvention, workforce development and substantial financial strengthening. The next tier of care for young people with more sustained and complex illness must be scaled up to support primary care. The evidence-based blueprints for these changes exist and will result in major returns on investment, greater than in any other domain of health care.

Mental health care must be financed, redesigned, staffed and nurtured to bring it up to the same standard as the rest of our health care system. The contrast between what is offered when someone is diagnosed with cancer or has a stroke, and when someone is experiencing an episode of a major mental illness, is stark. I have seen this contrast countless times in the same patient and within families, as family members develop either physical or mental disorders.

Why doesn't it happen?

"The crisis consists precisely in the fact that the old is dying and the new cannot be born."
Antonio Gramsci

When the facts are laid out and one reflects on how many people in Australia are acutely aware of this burgeoning need and lack of access to quality care, it is a mystery why reform doesn't happen. There is a huge band of suffering and anger simmering just below the surface in the community. Politicians should fear this, or ideally see the electoral opportunity in addressing it. Whether we regard it as a consequence of shame and stigma, a sense of helplessness and powerlessness, or lack of confidence in the value of mental health care and research, the public has not translated their genuine unmet need into activism, or a demand for action.

As with other major policy changes like the NDIS, there will be a need to organise the community to demand that this public health crisis and neglect is addressed. This will involve a combination of grassroots organising and effective and sustained political campaigning. One cannot rely on a fragmented mental health "sector" alone to deliver change. It is too easy to divide and rule as the elements in the "sector" represent vested interests, often conflicted through receipt of government funding, or are merely one element of the whole. The lack of this standing campaign with large numbers of grassroots community voices with a common set of demands seems to be the missing piece. Australians for Mental Health which I established in 2011 is one vehicle which has this goal front of mind. AfMH has recently started raising sufficient funds to secure real momentum and scale. If an assertive campaign can be fully realised, the crisis can be faced, and in the end "the new can be born".

Wage Growth is Good

Greg Jericho

Neoliberalism has so damaged our society that fear of wage growth now poisons almost all economic analysis and is an overriding determinant of economic policy.

So insidious has neoliberalism become that it is now considered quite sensible to state that lower wage growth and a smaller share of national income going to workers is a good thing. Indeed if you are to claim the opposite — that higher wages are good, that wages should grow faster than inflation, that workers deserve a greater share of the benefits of productivity, that wage growth has not been the main cause of inflation — then the full weight of Australia's official economic institutions, academy and most of the media will be brought to bear.

This was made abundantly clear when The Australia Institute used standard economic methodology to reveal that profits, not wages had driven inflation through 2022 and 2023. In response the Reserve Bank attacked the research and gave media organisations special briefings in an attempt to discredit the work.[1] Treasury officials branded the analysis as "flawed"[2] and one senior academic told the *Australian Financial Review* that the research should be withdrawn.[3]

And then the OECD and the IMF produced research that supported The Australia Institute.[4]

The assertion that wage growth was not causing inflation cut to the heart of the 40-year neoliberal project. Forty years of convincing people they should be content with lower wages, and slowly growing living standards. Forty years of convincing people that less union representation, less ability to strike and less ability to negotiate for higher wages was good for the economy. Forty years of convincing journalists that company profits are so important that companies should not have to reduce margins even during massive cost upheavals resulting from the COVID lockdowns and Russian invasion of Ukraine. Forty years of convincing Australians that profits are good because they lead to increased tax revenue, but that conversely, we should not tax those profits too greatly or companies will stop mining our gas and coal.

The full damage of this fear was made cruelly obvious in November 2022.

At that time Australians had experienced two years of collapsing real wages and were in the midst of 10 out of 11 quarters of wages failing to grow more than prices. By March 2023, the real value of wages had fallen 6% in less than three years. This was equivalent to a worker on average earnings of $75,000 losing $4,500. In just over two years, a decade's worth of increased living standards was wiped out. But in November 2022, the RBA did not focus on this, nor on surging profits.

Instead, in its November statement, the Reserve Bank announced it raised the cash rate because it was concerned about "avoiding a prices-wages spiral", and that it would "continue to pay close attention" to "labour costs and the price-setting behaviour of firms in the period ahead".[5] At this point real unit labour costs were 5.2% lower than they had been prior to the pandemic, while real unit profits cost were some 15.2%.

Of that nothing was said.

Workers had seen their living standards crumble and the response was worry from the Reserve Bank that they might recover that loss too quickly — or indeed at all.

Fear of wages is widespread. Each year business groups warn that wage rises, even for the lowest paid, will send companies to the wall. In 2024 the Australian Chamber of Commerce and Industry recommended the minimum wage rise by just 2% — much less than the 3.6% inflation at that time.[6]

This recommendation received no negative press, or suggestion that it risked damaging an economy already slowing due to weak household spending. But when wages grew 4.0% in the 12 months to September 2023 while inflation rose 5.4%, the *AFR* warned: "Wages growth hits 14-year high, fueling inflation fears."[67]

Yes, we should be worried that wages rising less than inflation might fuel inflation!

Such fears do not apply to wealth. When presenting its own "Richest 200 list", the *AFR* boasted "the fortunes of the Rich 200 swelled 11%".[8] And rather than warn about inflation, the paper editorialised that there is no "entrenched oligarchy that controls an ever-increasing share of the nation's wealth due to some Marxist law in which the return of capital exceeds the economy's growth rate".[9] They made this claim despite the 11% growth in wealth vastly exceeding the economy's growth rate at the time of 1.4%.

Often employer groups and conservatives will blame low wage growth on low productivity because theoretically productivity growth should lead to higher wages.[10] From 1991 to 2000, productivity grew 22% while real hourly earnings increased a similar 21%. And during this period the economy grew on average by 3.5%. But since then, things have shifted. Since 2000, productivity has increased 28% while real earnings per hour have risen just 12.5%. This is not how the economy is meant to operate. It's clear workers are owed nearly 25 years of back pay.

Wage growth should not be feared but welcomed and encouraged. Household spending makes up just over half of the entire economy and workers spend on average 85% of their disposable personal income. Stronger wage growth not surprisingly leads to more spending on consumer goods and services. Economist Jim Stanford estimated that a 2% stronger annual wage growth would add almost $355 billion to workers over five years most of which would be spent and create more jobs.[11]

Strong wage growth with workers getting the full benefits of productivity growth leads to a strong economy. We need to end the absurd and damaging policies driven by irrational fears of wage breakouts that never arrive. Wage growth is good, and real wage growth is necessary to lift everyone's living standards.

1   RBA (2023) RBAFOI-222347, https://www.rba.gov.au/information/foi/disclosure-log/rbafoi-222347.html
2   Treasury (2023) *Freedom of Information Release 3376*, https://treasury.gov.au/the-department/accountability-reporting/foi/3376
3   Mize (2023) "Australia Institute urged to retract 'flawed' profit-inflation report", *AFR*, https://www.afr.com/policy/economy/australia-institute-urged-to-retract-flawed-profit-inflation-report-20230513-p5d84j
4   OECD (2023) Economic Outlook, Vol 2023, Issue 1 https://www.oecd-ilibrary.org/economics/oecd-economic-outlook/volume-2023/issue-1_ce188438-en and IMF (2023) "Europe's Inflation Outlook Depends on How Corporate Profits Absorb Wage Gains", https://www.imf.org/en/Blogs/Articles/2023/06/26/

    europes-inflation-outlook-depends-on-how-corporate-profits-absorb-wage-gains
5   RBA (2022) "Statement by Philip Lowe, Governor: Monetary Policy Decision, November 2022" https://www.rba.gov.au/media-releases/2022/mr-22-36.html
6   FWC (2024) *Annual Wage Review 2023–24 Submissions*, https://www.fwc.gov.au/hearings-decisions/major-cases/annual-wage-reviews/annual-wage-review-2023-24/submissions-annual
7   Read and Marin-Guzman (2023) "Wages growth hits 14-year high, fueling inflation fears", *AFR*, https://www.afr.com/policy/economy/wages-growth-breaks-quarterly-record-to-hit-14-year-high-20231115-p5ek2f
8   Redrup and Bailey (2024), "Australia's wealthiest 200 now control $625b", *AFR*, https://www.afr.com/rich-list/australia-s-10-richest-people-revealed-20240521-p5jfe4
9   AFR (2024) "Ageing Rich Listers approach wealth dispersal watershed", https://www.afr.com/wealth/people/ageing-rich-listers-approach-wealth-dispersal-watershed-20240528-p5jh5g
10 See Marin-Guzman (2024) "Weak productivity halts minimum wage rise", *AFR*, https://www.afr.com/work-and-careers/workplace/minimum-wage-rises-3-75pc-in-line-with-inflation-20240603-p5jirj
11 Stanford (2023) "Stronger Wage Growth improves the Economy and the Budget", https://australiainstitute.org.au/post/stronger-wage-growth-improves-the-economy-and-the-budget/

The Price of Extinction

Bob Brown

In late 2023, Tasmania's Civil and Administrative Tribunal gave the go-ahead for a wind farm with skyscraper-height ailerons on Tasmania's Robbins Island on condition that a monetary "offset" or "financial contribution" of $100,000 be paid by the developers for each orange-bellied parrot the development kills. There were an estimated 74 orange-bellied parrots left in the wild, so the price of wiping out the species was set at $7.4 million. That's not saying the wind farm will kill all the orange-bellied parrots but it does put a dollar tag on the cost to the developer, ACEN, if it did.

To extrapolate a little, there are 1.2 million listed species on Earth but only 30,000 of these are animals, birds or reptiles. Roughly speaking, that means the whole animal kingdom, in Tasmanian tribunal values, is worth 30,000 times $7.4 million: a total of $222 billion or a tad less than Australia's future nuclear submarine fleet. Of course, you would have to wait for each species to get down to 74 before payments applied.

The $7.4 million extinction fee for the orange-bellied parrot should not be much of a bother for the Philippines' Ayala family corporation which owns ACEN, as *Forbes* lists the family's worth at $2.8 billion. So the parrot's continued existence on the planet is worth about one tenth of one per cent of the Ayala's family wealth.

The Robbins Island wind farm will sit astride the bird's narrow migratory path between Tasmania and mainland Australia.

The tribunal panel, Messrs Grueber, Loveday and Kitchell, also priced the death of each Tasmanian wedge-tail eagle killed by the wind farm at $100,000. The giant eagle's road to extinction is shortened by the logging of native forests for export woodchips as authorised by the Albanese Labor government in Canberra and former Liberal government in Hobart.

The tribunal's finding number 218 read:

> We also consider that an additional offset should be included as a contribution that mirrors the proposed condition for eagles, which is a $100,000.00 financial contribution for each detected eagle mortality. OBP mortalities are at least as significant as eagle mortalities and a similar condition should be provided for them.

This fits neatly with the plan by the Federal Minister for the Environment, Tanya Plibersek, to have Australia become the "Green Wall Street" of the world. Her government is working on legislation to monetise the environment. The pricing of nature indicates that every living thing can become tradeable and that, unavoidably, includes the human spirit and love of nature being discounted to zero. It is a materialist breakthrough in the gutting of humanity's historic relationship with our natural planet.

Everything, including our valuing of fellow species, forests, oceans and icecaps, can be monetised. This is echoed in the argument for keeping Newcastle as the world's largest coal export port: the Albanese government justifies it as bringing in $40 billion a year while discounting to zero its role in the future damage to the planet, including our human psyche, of a 3°C temperature rise and a 3-metre sea-level rise. It discounts the right of our children to a secure natural world and puts the incalculable monetary as well as psychological burden on them.

Naturally, the hundreds of people who have been arrested for peacefully blockading the port have come under sustained fire by the nation's political and business leaders. They are a cost to business.

The Tasmanian tribunal's decision received a ringing endorsement from both the Liberal and Labor parties. It is a pacemaker in the history of the deliberate dismantling of Earth's biosphere on the altar of capitalism. Vale the parrots and eagles who fly into the Ayala family's wind turbines. And, yes, that $100,000 "contribution" for each rare bird's death will be tax deductible.

Democratic Solidarity

Dr Emma Shortis

Following in the footsteps of many fixtures of far-right America, former Fox News turned independent commentator Tucker Carlson toured Australia in July 2024. Brought here by mining magnate Clive Palmer, Carlson found adoring audiences.

At an event in Canberra, Carlson attracted the expected figures from the Australian right, and a few sceptical journalists. Much was made of a "viral" moment in which he berated the Australian media. His audience, of course, loved it.

But Carlson is as slippery as he is ideological. At one point, he would no doubt have made that audience — a group of people deeply committed to the idea of American primacy and righteousness — rather uncomfortable.

Asked if China poses a threat to Australia, Carlson pivoted to the US–Australia alliance. He reflected on "the fears that have pushed generations of Australian governments into a counterproductive alliance with the United States and Great Britain". That enduring fear of hostile powers, Carlson continued, means that "the view here is that the US will rescue us if we ever really have a problem. And I don't think that's true. I'm sorry to say that … I just don't think it's true, and I think you're unwise for believing it's true."

Tucker Carlson has abhorrent views on most things. But on this point, he is right.

That even Carlson can see this truth should be a source of great embarrassment. The myth that the Americans will come to our rescue should we ever need them has endured for over 70 years, but it has always been just that — a myth.

The mythology of our security relationship with the United States stems, of course, from the experience of World War II and our "abandonment" by Great Britain. It was further ingrained by the 1951 ANZUS Treaty and the formalisation of the security alliance. But despite unsubstantiated claims to the contrary, the ANZUS Treaty promises us nothing — it gives only the assurance that both parties will "consult" when "political independence or security of any of the parties is threatened in the Pacific", "act to meet the common danger" and then to report to the UN Security Council "all measures taken as a result". All of this means nothing more nor less than what anyone wants it to mean.

Successive Australian governments' desperation to shore up this mythical security guarantee is what makes the alliance, as Carlson astutely observed, so counterproductive. It has drawn Australia into unnecessary and damaging wars reaching far beyond the Pacific, and created a unique kind of subservience. It is what gave us the indefensible AUKUS submarine pact.

Australian governments' deeply ingrained fears have led them to believe that Australia must stick to the United States no matter what it does, and no matter who is in charge — even if it is someone like Donald Trump.

At one particularly worrying point for American democracy, one Australian journalist even insisted that when it comes to the US alliance, "cosying up to a madman ... [is] a necessity".

But what if all of that failed, when and if it came down to it?

Or what if cosying up to madmen and handing them $368 billion and our sovereignty actually made things more dangerous for us, and our region? What if we listened to Tucker Carlson, and understood that Americans aren't coming to save us?

Or, even better, that we don't need saving?

That would not mean abandoning our alliance with the United States. It would mean changing the way it works, and how we understand it. It would mean dramatically rethinking what we mean when we talk about "security". In our counterproductive alliance with the United States, security seems to mean only the temporary absence of war that political and military leaders on both sides of the Pacific believe to be inevitable — war that can only be prevented by projections of military might.

Security, though, should mean a lot more than that. It should mean collective human flourishing — not just the absence of war, but genuine wellbeing grounded in equality and prosperity. That would mean identifying and working in genuine partnership on the things that do threaten us: climate change, nuclear proliferation, inequality. It would mean distinguishing between those genuine threats, and risks — like our relationships with great powers — to be managed.

A productive relationship with the United States would be grounded in democratic solidarity — not fear.

At times, that democratic solidarity might make for some uncomfortable conversations.

Democratic solidarity would mean focusing on transparency and accountability, and being consistent in those commitments — not something the alliance is particularly good at right now. But it is in Australian interests just as much as it is in American interests that American democracy survives and thrives.

Australia — as a thriving, though imperfect, democracy — has a lot to offer in that regard. And we know we can have those uncomfortable conversations and survive them. The Australian Government did that only recently, when it secured the release of Australian citizen Julian Assange. For a brief moment, the Australian Government demonstrated that it could advocate for its own interests and the interests of its citizens, while at the same time challenging Americans to see what is also in their best interests. Holding an Australian citizen hostage for publishing the truth was never in the interests of the most important democracy in the world.

Confronting the glaring hypocrisies of American power is difficult. But more than that, it is necessary. That was clearly demonstrated when, not long after Assange's release, the Biden administration secured the release of American journalists being held hostage in Russia — something that arguably could not have happened while such appalling treatment of an Australian citizen was allowed to stand.

Assange's release was a preview of what the US–Australian relationship might be, and how it is possible to advocate for our own interests without succumbing to fear or subservience.

Because we matter. We just have to accept that truth, and ask ourselves: what could we bring to the world if we weren't so afraid?

An Australian Peace and Security Strategy

Professor John Langmore AM

Peace and security are at the heart of what most Australians want from government, though not often articulated in that way. More commonly attention is focused on defence policy. In reality, though, voters are more concerned about incomes and employment, health, and education, living standards and leisure.

Of the four areas of foreign policy — diplomatic and trade relations, defence, intelligence and aid — Australian governments have been preoccupied with military and intelligence capacity, and neglectful of diplomacy and constructive developmental cooperation. This has seriously undermined our security. Expenditure on diplomacy as a proportion of total Commonwealth outlays was halved between 1995 and 2020. Aid has been cut so drastically that Australia has joined the meanest donors among wealthy countries, while military expenditure is exploding. Yet there is still no process in place for a comprehensive review.

Clarity about national objectives and policies requires consultation at all levels: democratic political representation; rigorous, expert bureaucratic review; cabinet discussions; comprehensive parliamentary committee assessment; opportunities for scholarly research; free journalism; consultation and community discussion. Prevention of such review and discussion, such as happened before the AUKUS decision was made, is autocratic manipulation.

Effective assessment must include identification of the full range of choices and the implications of each for economic, social, environmental and cultural goals. These are complex and difficult tasks. Fiscal calculations of the implications of each possibility are crucial because every government's financial resources are finite.

A necessary framework for wise decisions is a national strategy for achieving the goals. A country in which the national government recognises that the electorate prefers to live peacefully needs a national peace and security strategy. That strategy would identify the mechanisms for building trust and cooperation, nationally and internationally, which requires focusing on domestic policies for maximising wellbeing and international policies of multilateral cooperation.

Whatever the situation, the strategy must include possibilities for all forms of peacebuilding. These include diplomatic dialogue, formal negotiation, international mediation, multilateral review, arbitration, and legal action. A mature political process recognises the importance of alliances, but it also requires empathetic recognition that all countries seek autonomy and independent processes that reflect national interests. Such recognition normally offers opportunities for conflict-reducing compromises.

None of those stages were part of the AUKUS political process. Former Prime Minister Morrison claims improbably in his condescendingly titled book *Plans for Your Good* that AUKUS was his idea. His book describes an autocratic process focused on persuading the US White House and Pentagon to allow Australia to buy nuclear-powered submarines. Much of the preparation and negotiation was conducted by highly paid American advisors integrated within the Australian Defence Department. This explicitly illustrates the loss of sovereignty which AUKUS involves.

Under Foreign Minister Wong's questioning in a Senate Budget Committee, the Vice Chief of the Australian Defence Force admitted that the relative costs and benefits of the AUKUS proposal and its alternatives had never been rigorously evaluated by the Defence Department. The central inadequacy was that at no point was there ever a comprehensive, rigorous evaluation of alternative strategies for building security. There is no indication that alternative types of weapons were rigorously evaluated. If nuclear-powered submarines were judged to be desirable, why not change the terms of the contract with France and purchase some of theirs to avoid the betrayal of the contract with them?

The process was characterised by secrecy, delusion, and trickery. Labor shadow ministers were only told about the enormous project on the evening of 15 September 2021 before the 7 am public announcement on 16 September. Labor had been deliberately deceived. Labor had been wedged. This was only the first of Morrison's tricks. Another was deliberately misleading President Macron.

Even though Labor was initially supportive, after the election they could and should have set up a comprehensive review of security strategy. Wise policy making suggests this would still be of great value, and it would be one essential basis for an Australian Peace and Security Strategy.

Australia last had a National Security Strategy in 2013, under the previous Labor government. Many governments have such a strategy. A national Peace and Security Strategy recognises that policies interact. Defence can only be adequately evaluated with integration with other aspects of national security such as health, housing, education, climate, infrastructure, and research, which also have existential significance. A national objective of improving the wellbeing of all must include the major elements contributing to that national goal.

The fiscal consequences of the proposed package through the innumerable cuts and constraints to human services cannot be justified. Is Australian wellbeing improved more effectively by owning nuclear-powered submarines or by housing the homeless and contributing to peaceful, environmentally responsible development of the Australian population and of other countries in the region?

A central question for Australia is what military strategy should we adopt? Many wise military planners support national protection rather than forward assertiveness. The purchase of the nuclear-powered submarines will put Australian defence under American control. The abandonment of sovereignty is misguided because it increases the risks of being drawn by the US into more unwanted and irrelevant wars.

The enormous project is quite contrary to the global strategy the UN General Assembly advocates, and the negotiation of policies that are being prepared for the Summit of the Future in New York in September 2024. UN Secretary-General Guterres aims for agreement on a global strategy that constrains the accelerating international arms race and gives high priority to upgrading diplomacy everywhere and focusing on conflict prevention and peacebuilding.

So far Australia's response is relatively passive. Australian expenditure on diplomacy is now increasing, slowly, and so far, is doing little to recover from the neglect of the last quarter century. If we want other UN Member States to restrain their military spending and increase their diplomacy, we must do so too. It is vital that the Australian Government systematically reviews how to implement the Summit's conclusions and share in that implementation.

The majority of voters in most countries prefer peace to war. The growing unease about AUKUS in Australia is one aspect of this.

Governments that seek re-election will increase their support if they effectively contribute to reducing violent conflict. This can happen if they focus on peacebuilding. For this reason alone, the Labor government would do well to initiate preparation of an Australian Peace and Security Strategy, part of which would be to rigorously evaluate AUKUS — for the first time.

Caution is Killing Us

Polly Hemming

Australia is a country that seemingly has everything. One of the wealthiest countries in the world, we have peace, democratic stability, fresh air, clean water, abundant resources, and international influence. But for a country so privileged we also have some surprisingly big problems.

Australia is facing an equality crisis. Children are living in poverty. Women are being murdered by their partners. People living in residential care are malnourished. Indigenous incarceration and child removals are increasing. Australian governments are failing to uphold civil liberties and political freedoms.

And, of course, all this inequality is set against and exacerbated by the rapidly worsening climate and biodiversity crises caused by our collective determination to subsidise fossil fuel expansion and ravage our natural environment.

The problem is not money. The share of Australians' combined incomes going to corporate profits is well up, as are CEO salaries and fossil fuel subsidies. Our government just sacrificed $200 billion on tax cuts, and it is going to spend almost $400 billion on nuclear submarines we may or may not get.

This continent and its culture are ancient, but the colony of Australia is young. There is no need to trace back through millennia of successive empires to understand how we got here. None of our leaders has been forced into faustian pacts to save their citizens from starvation or tyranny. While the solutions to some of our problems are complex, it's not hard to see where to start, and what things need to stop. Our governments knew how to end whaling and asbestos mining, and they know today how to fix the big problems hitting Australians.

Despite our growing, collective abundance, Australia is facing a notable deficit in one thing: the courage to confront and fix these problems.

As our nation's prosperity has increased, complacency and caution has taken the place of boldness and bravery. With the rapid intensification of neoliberalism over the last 30 years, our leaders have sold us the myth that "doing the right thing" means taking care of number one, and providing for others means there will be less for us.

Increasingly, what follows a big policy announcement in Australia is not a big, structural solution but a series of incremental "announceables". Instead of systemic reform, a tired array of political tactics and interminable bureaucratic processes are typically dragged out: commissions, committees, strategies, reviews, consultations, economic modelling and endless cost-benefit analyses. When implemented in good faith, these processes should justify and facilitate policy changes, but in the current context they serve to delay or water down ambition. The result is the continued status quo of increasing inequality, injustices and environmental decline as millions stand by and watch.

The failure of successive leaders to communicate the gravity of the climate crisis and to do the most basic things climate scientists say are needed to sustain life as we know it — stop opening new gas and coal mines, stop clearing forests, and rapidly restore our ecosystems — is an abject and unforgivable demonstration of this performative inaction. Australian governments, senior public servants and industry leaders have known for decades what causes climate change and what its impacts will be. Yet ecosystem collapse is consistently treated as an economic inconvenience, rather than a moral imperative.

Much is made of the powerful grip industry and media oligarchs have on Australia's democracy. There is no doubt that the pursuit of profit and self-interest by a select few continues to have a disproportionate influence over our policymaking. But is it the identity or alleged "power" of these influential individuals that is important, or the failure of our leaders and public agencies and institutions to stand up to them?

We are all guilty of taking the path of least resistance or acting out of self-interest sometimes. We have all stood by when we could have done more because we wanted to avoid conflict or didn't want to lose social acceptance, financial stability or access to power. We've told ourselves we can make "change from inside" or convinced ourselves we are too small to make a difference.

Recent commissions into the Robodebt scheme, institutional child sexual abuse, government use of consultancies, to name just a few, have made acutely clear what the consequences of collective silence and inaction can be.

To quote Eleanor Roosevelt, "We do not have to become heroes overnight. Just one step at a time, meeting each thing that comes up, seeing it is not as dreadful as it appeared, discovering we have the strength to stare it down."

This is in no way to suggest Australians are bad people. Actually, we inherently want to do the right thing. While neoliberal economics has us convinced that individuals should and do act in their own self-interest, in fact, there is significant evidence to suggest that humans have an evolutionary and biological predisposition towards altruism, not selfishness.

Just as there is evidence pointing to the innate altruism of humans, there is also significant evidence demonstrating that humans preference morality over economics or efficiency when it comes to making big decisions. Of course, morality is subjective, but humans immortalise in history, religion, art and culture those who saved lives, sacrificed themselves and spoke truth to power. It's hard to recall a historical figure who has been celebrated for their centrism, fiscal pragmatism or techno-optimism.

Even former Prime Minister John Howard, a devout follower of the neoliberal doctrine, reinforced this theory at least once in his life. In response to the 1996 Port Arthur massacre, Howard negotiated aggressively with states, resisted the gun lobby, implemented a nationwide tax, and fought his own constituents and Coalition partners to introduce nation-changing gun laws and regulations, to ensure such a tragedy could never be repeated.

This is not to martyr or ignore the other significant harms that Howard went on to inflict on our nation after these first few months in office. But it shows just how quickly governments can make big things happen when they want to, even those who claim to believe in "small government". It also shows that Australians are willing to accept increased tax and regulatory burdens if it means saving lives.

The Port Arthur tragedy resulted in the deaths of 35 people and within months John Howard had passed laws to stop it happening again. No one attempted to bright-side the opportunities that gun laws would bring in growing the economy or creating investment and business "opportunities". No one suggested that weapons manufacturers should be consulted or be allowed to influence process. No consultants were commissioned to project job losses in the firearm industry.

Governments are remembered for what they did, not the economic modelling they commissioned. Indeed, Labor governments are remembered for implementing bold, nation-changing ideas in accordance with the principles of the Labor Party constitution: the abolition of poverty, the redistribution of economic and political power and the social ownership of natural resources.

The Whitlam government introduced Medibank, free tertiary education and passed historical sex- and disability-discrimination laws. The Hawke government gave us Medicare, convinced the world not to mine Antarctica and floated the Australian dollar. The Rudd government apologised to the survivors of the Stolen Generations and steered Australia through the global financial crisis with a public-spending package. And the minority Gillard government negotiated a carbon price with the Greens that successfully lowered emissions and created the NDIS.

But bravery is like a muscle, and it atrophies without use. At a time where our nation is facing its biggest problems, progressive politics appears to be characterised by caution, conflict aversion and the need for validation by the private sector more than ever before.

The modern Coalition doesn't seem to suffer from this affliction. While the current Labor government shrinks its ambitions to make itself as small a target as possible, the Coalition unapologetically proposes the reintroduction of government-owned power stations and a $600 billion nuclear-power industry.

That rapidly growing inequality and the worsening climate and biodiversity crisis is killing Australians should be enough of a reason for our governments to overcome their terror of being accused of fiscal negligence or economic recklessness.

In government and public institutions bravery means using the levers of power with integrity, even when others don't. It means doing what is required to fix problems, not just what is sufficient to avoid them. It means standing up to the party or those with perceived power. It means acting in the public interest. It means telling the truth.

The rest of us are not off the hook either, regardless of what industry we are in. If we claim to care about childhood poverty or violence against women or extinctions, then we must be brave enough to speak loud enough for our leaders to listen.

And if we aren't brave enough to take these steps — to change ourselves and our country — then let's hope we are brave enough to face the consequences that will come with doing nothing.

Confronting Reality in an Evolving Information and Communications Mediascape

Professor Peter Doherty AC

Since the advent of the internet and, beyond that, social media, we have been living through a time of extraordinary transformation. For instance, as a research scientist, I no longer walk to a university library to access journal articles but read everything online. That's great in many ways, but one downside is that I don't take a break to browse the library shelf of paper periodicals (like *Nature* or *Science*) that publish in-depth research articles (or excellent news and views summaries) on important and intriguing topics that can be far from my own area of expertise. The consequence is that, facilitated by the channelling effects of web browsers and social media, my intellectual world can unconsciously narrow.

Fortunately, the web also offers everything necessary to sustain a broad world view. We can subscribe to great daily (*The New York Times*) and weekly (*The Economist*) generalist publications, where we see the best of journalism. An excellent, local alternative to being poisoned each day by reading some Australian newspapers is to start the morning by scanning the list of content for *The Conversation*. Just sign up, and it will be delivered free to your email. I'm proud of the fact that I played a small part in helping former newspaper editor Andrew Jaspan (with the backing of then University of Melbourne Vice-Chancellor Glyn Davis) get *The Conversation* up and running. Andrew's idea of publishing 800-word generalist articles from academics — after editing for readability via a newsroom of professional journalists — has gone global. Various regional versions of *The Conversation* now provide quality content across the planet, with Melbourne remaining "mission central". Many great articles you might read in other outlets are republished free (under Creative Commons) from *The Conversation*.

Then there's the two-way discussion facilitated by social media. My involvement with Twitter (now X) increased massively from the December 2019 onset of COVID-19, as I tried to communicate what seemed like good information and answer people's questions in my area: infection and immunity. Soon, I also found myself dealing with a spectrum of anonymous abuse and the weird distortions of conspiracy theories that were coming from across the planet. That communication can be painful, but it has value. Robust confrontation helps to prick any pomposity and, hopefully, engage a wide audience beyond the world of nuance, evidence and reason that should define the scientific life. Though social media is generally better handled by the young, we should all feel free to say our piece while, at the same time, be prepared to understand different world views and, if they are dangerous, try to counter them.

Anyone who researches anything is very aware that the internet allows extraordinary access to good information (my first look at a new topic may start with Wikipedia) and, during COVID at least, the pre-X iteration of Twitter allowed professionals to link up and share insights and new data in close to real time. The downside of the internet is, of course, that it also allows the dissemination of confected absurdities and deliberate lies. And it provides a mechanism for those who look constantly for someone (rather than something) to blame and reinforce ever weirder and more dangerous ideas. As a lab researcher and a disease and death guy (a pathologist), it never fails to amaze me that many of us seem to find the idea that (as Tony Abbott so succinctly summarised) "shit happens" to be unacceptable.

We can't, it seems, be part of nature and at the mercy of nature. In "conspiracy world" a pandemic must be blamed on "evil people" (not us of course) with the implication that, by identifying them, we will find solutions. Rubbish, of course, but that's how some see the human experience. Any sane approach to life acknowledges that people and governments make mistakes: SNAFUs are an old and enduring phenomenon. But if we want to get somewhere with unwelcome realities like a pandemic, or the progressive disruption caused by climate change, demonising others provides neither insight nor remedy.

The reality is that we must do the hard yards, work out what is really happening, be prepared to say so clearly and publicly, and find solutions. That's what science ideally does: first identify the problem then probe and develop solutions. It will, I believe, be only a matter of time before the conspiracy theorists work out some way to blame the climate scientists, who have been doing everything possible to warn us about the extreme danger of continuing down our present path, for causing climate change! And they will be supported by degraded elements in the online, print and broadcast media!

With no training or prior experience, I've been involved in public science communication since 1997 when, as a US resident and Australian of the Year (the selection process was different back then) my wife and I crossed the Pacific several times to speak to general audiences in all the capital cities. We met great Australians and realised there was a very real need for more scientists to be involved in public communication. John Howard was PM. I met with him several times. His politics aren't my politics, but I appreciated that he was genuinely interested in science and greatly increased the funding of the Australian Research Council and the National Health and Medical Research Council during his time in office. Which brings me to my final point.

As I've increasingly become aware since returning to Australia in 2002, we are privileged to live in one of the most robust democracies on the planet. The obvious consequence is that, if we want to see science-based policy in areas that deal with the natural world, we need to do our utmost to engage with every voter. Since 2005, I've published seven books on science and the scientific life, generated 120 consecutive blogposts during COVID[1] and have, at times, been very active via broadcast and print media. But there's the problem.

I have the sense that people like me are talking to at best 20% of the population. From my distant Methodist upbringing, we preach to the converted! How do we move beyond that? Talk-back radio offers one mechanism: my experience with program hosts has been great. We must be sophisticated in our use of social media. Organisations need to employ young people to target that area specifically. Like Al Gore's Climate Reality Project, we need to build networks of community influencers. We can't ignore what's happening now in the US. We can't let our public discourse be dominated by fear, hate and lies. We need to shout: "Great is truth and mighty above all things!"[2]

1   Doherty (2020–2024), https://www.doherty.edu.au/news-events/setting-it-straight
2   *King James Bible* 1 Esdras, 4:41

Politics is Good

Bill Browne

If a flying saucer landed in the rose gardens at the Museum of Australian Democracy and we offered to take the passengers to see our leaders at Parliament House, the aliens might reasonably ask how Australian leaders are chosen.

The walk down Centenary Trail to Parliament House would allow time to outline how our parliamentary, representative democracy works: Australians choose one person from every 100,000 or so adult citizens to represent us all and vote on our behalf to decide if new laws should be made or not. Every few years, we get the chance to choose a new representative if the old one isn't up to scratch.

The aliens would be suitably impressed. "Only one human chosen from one hundred thousand — you must truly adore, admire and love these chosen few."

"Love them? We don't even like them!"

But are our fellow citizens really so naïve, selfish and easily led that they choose only liars, cheats and frauds from the 100,000 citizens in each electorate?

Interrogated by an outsider, the old certainties might fall away. Perhaps we would concede that politicians are, as a class, no worse than those who voted for them, and maybe even a measure smarter, wiser and more civic-minded.

Why do we imagine that Australians chosen at random — on a citizens' jury, for example — would make better decisions about policy than professionals who serve at the pleasure of those same citizens?

Having served on a citizens' jury myself, I was painfully aware of how much better my decision-making could have been if I'd been employed full-time, with staff, access to the Parliamentary Library, and a few years' or decades' political experience under my belt. In short, I think I would have been in a better position to make decisions if I'd been a career politician.

Speechwriter Dennis Glover, reflecting on Mark Latham's short-lived rejection of politics back in 2004, said: "In a democracy, contesting power is a legitimate vocation."

Imagine if we treated the role of parliamentarian as a legitimate, and indeed essential, role in a democracy. Imagine if we spoke about, and to, candidates seeking election to Parliament as if they were pursuing a worthy occupation. Maybe we would find ourselves more sympathetic to them, and with a better understanding of the art of politics to boot.

At its heart, politics involves building and mobilising a constituency for change. Politicians are more susceptible to pressure, to the shifts in constituencies, than they are to facts or "evidence-based policy". While that might frustrate some with strong views about the role of evidence, it is important to highlight that the word evidence is not actually mentioned in the Constitution.

We have a representative democracy, and our representatives are responsive to the demos, the people. Such a statement of fact is no doubt uncomfortable for those whose currency is facts and figures, but it is hardly grounds for concluding that "politics is broken". Democracy is working, even when it isn't working the way everyone would like.

As Canberra insiders say, "Every time Parliament sits, someone leaves happy". It is an uncomfortable thought to sit with. Why are some groups and constituencies so much more successful than others at changing the country? Stripped of the old scapegoats of dirty money, faceless men and cosy deals, we might conclude that our opponents are beating us because they are smarter, harder working and braver than we give them credit for. Perhaps, too, they take politics more seriously than we do — and show it more respect.

It is true that MPs are attentive — even deferential — to some lobby groups, vested interests and entrenched power. But even then, it is often the sway (or perceived sway) that those groups have on the thinking of the public that gives them their influence. I assure you it is not their political donations, since even the largest corporate donations are tiny compared to major party revenues.

Groups that win show iron will, consistency of purpose and a willingness to use all the tools available in a liberal democracy. By contrast, how often have their civil society rivals hesitated instead of pressing the advantage? Or an NGO preferred their access to powerful decision-makers over holding those decision-makers' feet to the fire? There are some experts and commentators who would rather be Cassandras than dirty their hands to stop their dark predictions from coming to pass. The "politics is broken" framing is a salve for these do-nothings just as it is a shroud for the doings of the worst politicians.

Sandwiched between the fascists and the Soviets while fighting in the Spanish Civil War, George Orwell observed that, "To say first 'Democracy is a swindle', and then 'Fight for democracy!' is not good tactics."

Nor is it good strategy to leave politics to the venal, the spiteful and the power-hungry. Dismissing all politicians as cast from the same mould is a gift to the bad ones.

This sympathetic lens does not mean we should let politicians — the chosen few, the one-in-a-hundred-thousand — off the hook. It means asking more of them. Elevating our politicians would only make a fall from grace more wounding.

Nor would a newfound respect for the art of politics make things comfortable for its practitioners. On the contrary, it would encourage competitors to muck in. Freed of the idea that politics corrupts, others might decide to build constituencies and apply more pressure of their own. These movements should be reality-based, but with the people hearing the facts and the politicians feeling the pressure, not the other way around.

This book collects dozens of big ideas, but without politics, without democracy, all ideas are inert. People can adorn themselves with ideas and values to express their personality, to revel in their cleverness, or to show others the kind of person that they are. But it is political action that will quicken those ideas, give them form and motion. If you, dear reader, are not willing to contest power for the sake of the ideas in this book, then you will cede the political debate to those who value their ideas more.

Australia's Role in Ridding the World of Nuclear Weapons

Hon Melissa Parke

In an impassioned speech at the Labor Party's national conference in Adelaide in December 2018, Anthony Albanese described nuclear weapons as "the most destructive, inhumane and indiscriminate weapons ever created". "Today," he said, "we have an opportunity to take a step towards their elimination."[1]

Referencing the party's long history of action on disarmament, he urged delegates to support a draft motion that would commit a future Labor government to signing and ratifying the Treaty on the Prohibition of Nuclear Weapons (TPNW), a landmark accord negotiated one year earlier at the United Nations in New York.

"I don't argue that this is easy," he continued. "I don't argue that it's simple. But I do argue that it's just." The motion, which he had initiated, was adopted with unanimous support and resounding applause.

Six years later, Albanese is prime minister and the TPNW is binding international law, having attained the 50 ratifications needed for its entry into force. Many of Australia's neighbours, including New Zealand, Malaysia, the Philippines, Thailand and Fiji, are counted among its states parties.[2] But we are still not on board.

Australia has always had a complicated relationship with "the bomb". In the early days of the nuclear age, the Menzies government allowed Britain to test its atomic arsenal in the South Australian desert and off the coast of Western Australia. A dozen full-scale tests were carried out, along with several hundred so-called "minor trials", dispersing radioactive particles across the entire continent.

The impact on Indigenous communities living downwind of the test sites at Maralinga and Emu Field was especially devastating. According to a 1985 royal commission, "The resources allocated for Aboriginal welfare and safety were ludicrous, amounting to nothing more than a token gesture."[3] To this day, vast swathes of land remain unsafe for habitation.

The Menzies government also tried without success to purchase nuclear bombs from Britain, and Australia's ambition of becoming a nuclear-armed state continued under the Gorton government, which pursued construction of a nuclear power plant at Jervis Bay, with bomb-making in mind.

But the Non-Proliferation Treaty (NPT) of 1968 put an end to Australia's nascent nuclear weapon program. At the United States' urging, Gorton reluctantly signed the agreement in 1970, though he refused to ratify it. Ratification would only occur three years later under Whitlam.

While Australia gave up its plan to acquire nuclear weapons, it did not give up on the idea of "nuclear protection" altogether. It sought assurances from the United States that it would use its nuclear forces in Australia's defence should the need arise. Whether such assurances were ever formally made remains unclear, but since the 1990s successive Australian governments have declared our country's reliance on America's so-called "nuclear umbrella".

This dangerous and absurd concept (dangerous because it makes Australia a nuclear target; absurd because the US would never sacrifice one of its own cities for ours) has severely restrained Australia's advocacy for a nuclear-weapon-free world. How can we credibly argue that nuclear weapons must be eliminated while asserting, in the same breath, that they guarantee our security and prosperity?

In 2008, when I was a Labor parliamentarian in the Rudd government, Australia and Japan established the International Commission on Nuclear Non-Proliferation and Disarmament, a follow-up to Keating's Canberra Commission on the Elimination of Nuclear Weapons. This important initiative, spearheaded by the former Foreign Minister Gareth Evans, aimed to galvanise global support for a long-neglected cause.

But behind the scenes, Australia advised the United States that its desire to support the commission's goals "must be balanced against our strategic interest in ensuring stability through ensuring a credible US extended deterrence", and our officials would enthusiastically endorse the continued modernisation of US nuclear forces.[4]

Today the "nuclear umbrella" remains in place and is the principal impediment to Australia becoming a TPNW state party. The Albanese government, in its national defence strategy of April 2024, stated: "Australia's best protection against the increasing risk of nuclear escalation is US extended nuclear deterrence and the pursuit of new avenues of arms control."[5]

Australia's long-standing support for US nuclear weapons is not merely rhetorical; it also has practical dimensions. Most notably, Pine Gap, the US military and intelligence facility near Alice Springs in central Australia, plays a role in US nuclear command and control — a role that would need to end if Australia is to become compliant with the TPNW.

The AUKUS military partnership between Australia, the United Kingdom and the United States, announced in 2021, has further diminished Australia's credibility as a non-proliferation advocate — although the pact does not appear to contradict any of the TPNW's provisions directly.

Under AUKUS, Australia hopes to acquire conventionally armed, nuclear-powered submarines, to be fuelled with highly enriched uranium, the essential ingredient for nuclear bombs. This poses a major challenge for the non-proliferation regime and would set a dangerous precedent for others to follow. Neighbouring countries have understandably responded with alarm and anger at the prospect of the greater nuclearisation of our region.

If the planned acquisition occurs — and there are serious doubts as to whether it will — it would be all the more imperative for Australia to join the TPNW, as this would provide additional guard rails against nuclear weapons, applicable to the current government and future governments. The TPNW prohibits a broader range of activities than the NPT and the 1985 South Pacific Nuclear Free Zone Treaty, to which Australia is already a state party.

Australia is also contributing to nuclear dangers by exporting several thousand tonnes of uranium each year. Recipients of our fissile material have included Russia, China, India and other nuclear-armed states. Australia's early exports were used to make US and British nuclear bombs. While today's exports are subject to international safeguards aimed at preventing diversion to weapons, they still carry unacceptable risks.

A different path for Australia is possible and necessary. A path that prioritises investments in peace and diplomacy over weapons and war, one that avoids further harm to people and the environment. To become a champion of nuclear disarmament, as Australia has long claimed to be, we must end our complicity in the perpetuation of global nuclear dangers.

The most obvious first step would be to act upon Labor's promise of signing and ratifying the TPNW, which establishes a comprehensive, globally applicable ban on the worst weapons of mass destruction. Australia's adherence to this landmark UN treaty would be an important contribution towards addressing one of the greatest threats facing humanity and our planet.

Today, there are more than 12,000 nuclear weapons at dozens of locations around the world, and the risk of their use appears to be increasing, not diminishing. Australia should stand with the global majority of nations in rejecting such weapons outright, not just for Russia or China or North Korea, but for everyone without exception.

In addition to providing a legal framework for the verified elimination of nuclear weapons, the TPNW includes novel provisions for assisting communities harmed by nuclear use and testing. In this regard, it is of particular importance to Indigenous Australians, who still live with the toxic legacy of the British tests conducted on their soil, and to our neighbours in the Pacific, where more than 300 US, British and French tests were carried out.

We must do everything in our power, as a nation, to ensure that these most horrific weapons are never used or tested again — for our security and every country's security. Just as Australia has joined treaties prohibiting chemical and biological weapons, antipersonnel land mines and cluster munitions, we must now join the international ban on "the most destructive, inhumane and indiscriminate weapons ever created".

1 Albanese (2018), https://anthonyalbanese.com.au/speech-moving-support-for-the-nuclear-weapon-ban-treaty-tuesday-18-december-2018
2 Treaty on the Prohibition of Nuclear Weapons (2017), https://treaties.un.org/Pages/ViewDetails.aspx?src=TREATY&mtdsg_no=XXVI-9&chapter=26&clang=_en
3 British Nuclear Tests in Australia – Royal Commission (1985), https://parlinfo.aph.gov.au/parlInfo/search/display/display.w3p;query=Id%3A%22

publications%2Ftabledpapers%2FHPP032016010928%22
4   Flitton (2011), https://www.smh.com.au/national/anti-nuclear-rudd-urged-us-to-keep-arsenal-for-deterrence-20111113-1ndw2.html
5   "2024 National Defence Strategy and 2024 Integrated Investment Program", https://www.defence.gov.au/about/strategic-planning/2024-national-defence-strategy-2024-integrated-investment-program

Curiosity-driven Research

Professor Brian Schmidt AC

Let's invest in the curiosity that brings big ideas, and have the confidence to use and share what we have learned to change Australia and the world for the better. We live in a time of short-term utilitarianism — where we struggle to think beyond the immediate and plan and invest for the long term. Yet the wicked challenges that humanity faces, such as achieving global sustainability or ensuring technology enhances rather than displaces lives, require ideas well outside of the current realm of thinking. History has shown that it is the ideas from blue-sky thinking driven by our innate curiosity that have provided solutions to the challenges to civilisations. It is curiosity-driven research, followed up by pragmatic application of our gained knowledge, that provides the effective technologies, policies and ideas that revolutionise our world, and enable us to navigate previously impossible problems.

On 30 May 1988, Prime Minister Hawke made the memorable aspiration "No longer content to be just the lucky country, Australia must now become the clever country!" and the notion of us being the Clever Country has rung through government circles ever since. So, how have we done? Hawke, consistent with most things under his prime ministership, delivered — raising the government investment in R&D from 0.56% of GDP in the 1988–89 Budget to 0.72% of GDP in the 1992–93 Budget. From that height in 1992-93, the trend has been downward such that in 2022–23, government investment in R&D had dropped to 0.49% of GDP, the lowest level since its measurement began in 1978. This fall is just the tip of a rather sad iceberg for basic research. From 1992 to 2020, Australia's investment in pure basic research dropped from 40% of the government's total research spend to 19%, with the combination of pure and strategic basic research dropping over the same period from 64% to 37%.

Curiosity-driven basic research has delivered for Australia and the world over the past decades. Peter Doherty and Rolf Zinkernagel's Nobel Prize-winning work on T-cells is the basis of previously impossible cancer treatments. Ian Frazier's work in creating the Gardasil HPV vaccine is now saving thousands of lives each year, and has been a major financial success for both CSL and the University of Queensland. CSIRO Astronomy's development of wi-fi has changed the world and the way we communicate. UNSW's development of PERC solar is the number one means by which humanity is taking on the challenge of reducing our greenhouse gas emissions.

UNSW famously could not get Australian investment in PERC. While the CSIRO did receive royalties for wi-fi, which were used to create the Science and Industry Endowment Fund, these were modest compared to the profits of the US tech giant, CISCO, that purchased the spinout company Radiata that created the technology to deliver wi-fi. We need to do much better at ensuring that we get more of the financial returns to stay in Australia from the knowledge we create. But unless we create more knowledge, venture capital will be less interested in investing the time, energy and money in Australian ideas.

Investing in curiosity-driven research is not just about making

Australians rich, it is about improving the prospects for humanity. We should celebrate the global impact our ideas have had — even the few examples listed here have enriched our lives well beyond the profits that might have been captured at home. Curiosity-driven basic research's value is often invisible, because it is the ideas from many discoveries that come together to make new technologies and ways of organising human societies possible. The most influential discoveries are surprises that advance our knowledge of the way the world works. Researchers often need to invent new tools in the process. It is the accumulation of tested ideas and the development of tools — the accumulation of knowledge — that is the feedstock for productivity growth.

There are also spillovers that percolate through our society at scale. Innovation is accelerated and productivity gets a boost when research graduates bring new skills, knowledge and networks to business and government. It is the ideas in public health or in economic policy that increase longevity and increase our prosperity. It's the ideas that are the basis of other ideas, that change the world. The spillovers from basic research are notoriously hard to quantify, but the economics literature is strongly of the view that the spillovers are large around the world. Elnasri and Fox confirmed this to be true in their economic analysis of the Australian economy in 2015. And just because spillovers are hard to measure and take much longer than the political cycle to materialise, does not mean they should be ignored by government with a cynical shrug of the shoulders and a muttering of "this won't help us win the next election".

Australia's future prosperity and our sovereign security are at stake. The US and China increasingly invest substantially more of their GDP in research than does Australia; the reason is they see it as critical to the trajectory of their power and wealth.

The Albanese government has set a long-term target of R&D

spending to reach 3% of GDP — but rather than making progress towards this target, government expenditure (as well as business expenditure) has gone backwards. It is only university R&D spending funded by international students that has increased — and with recent policy changes, this is sure to go backwards too.

Because of its long-term sovereign importance, R&D spending should not be a partisan issue. Investing in R&D is one of the few uncontested issues for the US Congress, despite the hyper-polarisation of US politics. A long-term R&D expenditure program needs to include the whole ecosystem, from curiosity-driven basic research, translational programs, and programs targeting increasing the capacity and sophistication of business. The program should be evidence-based, focus on market failure, have a stable 10-year outlook, and avoid at all costs the opportunity for the funding to be used as political pork barrelling.

R&D programs need stability to be effective. Shifting priorities to reflect the political hot-button issue of the day, or cutting programs to meet a budget target, undermine Australia's short- and long-term ability to generate knowledge and build the skills of our population.

Our current short-term strategy ignores the long-term degradation of our nation. Yes, it's true voters will not immediately notice the inability to recruit talent into our universities, the CSIRO and businesses. The loss of technical capability that forms our sovereign capability in defence, communications and remote sensing, for example, will hardly be seen over an election cycle. The tech start-ups that don't occur in the future will not make news. The absence of the wonder and discovery within our classrooms will not be an event, and nor will the ongoing decline in the number of Australians pursuing science and maths as career paths be reversed. The lower productivity of the country will cause a shrug of the shoulders — as already happens each year that the numbers are released. And future Australian Nobel Laureates, well — like in the old days — will just be those who have moved overseas to do their work.

Afterword

Dr Richard Denniss

Economists are notorious for making ridiculous predictions and, as a result, I don't make many predictions. I am, however, happy to predict the inevitable and, in turn, I'm very happy to predict that in the next 30 years Australia, and the world, will change dramatically.

How do I know this? Because the world is always changing, and the combination of the current rates of technological change, climate change and demographic change occurring make it inevitable that our societies, economies and natural environments will all change.

Change doesn't just happen; it is driven by people. The Berlin Wall didn't fall; it was knocked over. Likewise, whaling, asbestos mining and apartheid in South Africa didn't end; they were ended by brave, passionate, generous, determined people.

Neoliberalism's best trick is to convince us that markets, rather than people, shape the world. But markets are, literally, just a place where buyers and sellers come together. And since buyers and sellers are people, what neoliberalism really does is change the way that we think about how people, and which people, change the world. Talking up the power of "market forces" is designed to distract us from the power of democratic forces.

Its second-best trick is to train people to look for individual causes of, and solutions to, problems that are clearly structural in nature. The RBA uses interest rates to keep unemployment high enough to keep inflation low enough, but the unemployed are still blamed for their plight. Likewise, individuals are encouraged to recycle to protect the environment while state and federal governments spend more than $14 billion per year subsiding the extraction and use of fossil fuels.

And its third trick is to combine the first two to create a sense of hopelessness, cynicism and division. Even though Australia is one of the richest countries in the world, the thrall that neoliberalism has on this country means that a majority of Australians believe either that "the market" won't let us have good health or education systems, that our governments can't run good systems anyway, or most effectively of all, that those who want more spent on better health, education, transport and environmental policies need to fight among themselves for the scarce tax dollars. The very dollars made scarce by decades of tax cuts by those who oppose those goals for a better society.

But our history, that of Australia and of the Australia Institute, shows that progressive change is not only possible, but popular and, in turn, a powerful agenda around which to unite. Back in the 1990s, the Institute's research was making the case for broader measures of wellbeing than GDP, for big investments in renewable energy and a progressive tax system, while making the case against the privatisation of electricity. After decades of work, Australia now has a wellbeing framework for the Budget and a big and growing renewable-energy industry. The Australia Institute played a key role in stopping the Coalition's proposed company tax cuts and shifted $80 billion of the Stage 3 tax cuts from the top 20% to low- and middle-income earners. Back in 1999, our research helped prevent the full privatisation of the ACT's electricity and water assets and today the Victorian and Queensland governments are investing significantly in publicly owned energy assets.

Change is inevitable. It's the direction and pace of the change that is up for grabs, and it's that pace and direction that the Australia Institute's research is designed to influence.

The Institute began highlighting the need for a federal corruption watchdog back in 2016, and at the time we were criticised by both those who said it was too ambitious and those who said it wasn't necessary. By the 2022 election even the Coalition agreed, in principle, with the need for such a body.

At the Australia Institute our motto is "research that matters", but my favourite one-liner about what we do is "make the radical seem reasonable". Just as it seemed crazy to some to think that federal Parliament would ever create a body to investigate corruption at the national level, many think it's crazy to think that Australia will ever:

- stop building new fossil fuel projects;
- get a fair deal from the resource projects we do have;
- invest so much in pubic housing that living in such houses seems normal;
- create effective truth in political advertising laws; or
- abandon the absurdity of the AUKUS nuclear submarine deal.

But in 30 years' time such a list won't look radical; indeed it will likely look small and out of date.

I'm 54 and I've been involved in public policy my whole life. My first job after uni was at a think tank called the Evatt Foundation and since then I've worked as an academic, political adviser, researcher, consultant and company director. It took me 10 years to figure out that it takes 10 years to change something big, and I'm lucky to have been in the game long enough to have worked on enough wins to know that my losses weren't inevitable.

If "market forces" were all-powerful then how come the Coalition's company tax cuts were stopped in the Senate, the Stage 3 tax cuts were so radically redirected away from those with the most, and a federal corruption watchdog was created? If the fossil fuel industry was all-powerful inside Parliament House, then why are they spending so much money on advertising telling us how they are the "backbone" of our economy?

Democracy is not a movie. Happy endings aren't inevitable. In fact, there is no ending. Democracy is a daily grind, a game of inches, a play with no final act. At The Australia Institute we know that big change is possible, but we also know it's only possible if you put in the hard work.

On behalf of all the past, present and future staff of The Australia Institute it is an honour to say thank you to 30 years of volunteer board members, donors and supporters who make it possible for us to wake up in the morning and do the multifaceted research, communications, events and advocacy work required to make the radical seem reasonable.

Big change will happen in the next 30 years, and instead of hoping for positive change we will work to make it happen.

Contributor Biographies

Louise Adler's entire professional life has been in the cultural sphere as a board member, CEO and artistic director. She was CEO and Publisher at Melbourne University Press from 2008 to 2019 and she is currently the Director of Adelaide Writers' Week.

Pat Anderson is an Alyawarre woman known nationally and internationally as an advocate for the rights and health of Australia's First Nations people. She has extensive experience in Aboriginal health, community development, policy formation and research ethics. She was appointed an Officer of the Order of Australia (AO) in 2014 for distinguished service to the Indigenous community as a social justice advocate and was most recently recognised by the Women's International League for Peace and Freedom (WILPF). Ms Anderson was Co-Chair of the Referendum Council and together with Professor Megan Davis led the work of the Uluru Dialogue in partnership with the Indigenous Law Centre of the University of NSW.

Maiy Azize is the national spokesperson for Everybody's Home, a campaign to fix Australia's housing crisis. She is also the Deputy Director of Anglicare Australia, a network of welfare organisations linked to the Anglican church. Maiy has authored many reports and studies, including "Written Off: The High Cost of Australia's Unfair Tax System" for Everybody's Home and "Asking Those Who Know: A Study of Australians on Centrelink Payments" for Anglicare

Australia. She has also contributed to research on housing and poverty for the Australian Housing and Urban Research Institute, and serves as a Fellow at the Australian Basic Income Lab.

Allan Behm is advisor on The Australia Institute's International and Security Affairs program. He has had a career spanning nearly 30 years in the Australian public service. He was Chief of Staff to Minister for Climate Change and Industry, Greg Combet (2009–13) and senior advisor to the Shadow Minister for Foreign Affairs, Senator Penny Wong (2017–19). He has written three books: *No Minister*; *No Enemies No Friends* and *The Odd Couple*.

Bob Brown, environmentalist, doctor and former politician, is an environmental campaigner and former Parliamentary Leader of the Australian Greens. Born in Oberon, New South Wales, he moved to Tasmania in 1972, where he worked as a GP. He spent a decade in the Tasmanian House of Assembly as the Member for Denison and was elected to the federal Senate as a member of the Tasmanian Greens in 1996. He later joined West Australian Greens Senator Dee Margetts in founding the Australian Greens. He has written several books including his memoirs *Memo for a Saner World* (2004) and *Optimism* (2014). After stepping down as leader of the Greens and retiring from the Senate in 2012, he established the Bob Brown Foundation, a not-for-profit organisation supporting environmental causes.

Bill Browne is Director of the Democracy & Accountability Program at The Australia Institute. His diverse areas of interest include the use of opinion polling, forecasting to predict policy outcomes, truth in political advertising reforms, digital technology and the role of the states and the Senate in Australian democracy. Prior to coming to The Australia Institute, he worked as an environmental, social, governance (ESG) analyst.

Dr Richard Denniss, Executive Director of The Australia Institute, is a prominent Australian economist, author and public policy commentator, and has spent the last 20 years moving between policy-focused roles in academia, federal politics and think tanks. He was also a Lecturer in Economics at the University of Newcastle and former Associate Professor in the Crawford School of Public Policy at the ANU. He is a regular contributor to *The Monthly* and the author of several books including *Econobabble*; *Curing Affluenza* and *Dead Right: How Neoliberalism Ate Itself and What Comes Next*.

Professor Peter Doherty AC shared the 1996 Nobel Prize in Medicine with Swiss colleague Rolf Zinkernagel for their discoveries about transplantation and "killer" T-cell-mediated immunity, an understanding that is currently translating into new cancer treatments. The first veterinarian to win a Nobel, he was Australian of the Year in 1997. Still active in research on immunity to influenza, he commutes between St Jude Children's Research Hospital, Memphis and the Peter Doherty Institute at the University of Melbourne, where he now spends most of his professional time. Passionate about promoting an evidence-based view of reality, his most recent book is *The Knowledge Wars*. It suggests how any thoughtful citizen can bypass the facile propagandists and probe the scientific evidence for and against some of the big issues, like climate change or GM foods.

Dr Joëlle Gergis is an award-winning climate scientist and writer. She is an internationally recognised expert in Australian and Southern Hemisphere climate variability and change and has authored over 130 scientific publications. Joëlle served as a lead author on the latest United Nations' Intergovernmental Panel on the Climate Change's *Sixth Assessment Report* — a global review of climate-change science. Alongside her research activities, Joëlle has also published three highly-acclaimed general audience books: *Sunburnt Country: The History and Future of Climate Change in Australia*; *Humanity's Moment: A Climate Scientist's Case for Hope*; and *Highway to Hell: Climate Change and Australia's Future*. Joëlle was The Australia Institute's 2024 Writer In Residence.

Associate Professor Rebecca Glauert is the Director of the Australian Child and Youth Wellbeing Atlas, and the Scientific Director of the Raine Study, in the School of Population and Global Health at the University of Western Australia. Rebecca is committed to the use of data for public good and has dedicated her research career to connecting data-informed evidence to life-changing interventions for vulnerable citizens. She specialises in linking administrative datasets to explore the life-course epidemiology of health and wellbeing.

Polly Hemming is Director of The Australia Institute's Climate & Energy program. She has extensive experience working in both the not-for-profit and public sectors. Having previously led the development of a government eco-label recognising voluntary climate action by the private sector, she maintains a strong interest in non-state climate ambition and the policies and regulation that interact with this. Polly's previous roles have included academic publishing, remote Indigenous education, refugee advocacy and science communication.

José Ramos-Horta was Timor-Leste's first foreign minister when it declared independence from Portugal in 1975. Following Indonesia's invasion later that year, he became the international voice of the Timorese people. In 1996 he was awarded the Nobel Peace Prize. When Timor-Leste became a new nation following the Popular Consultation of 1999, he returned from exile to serve as the new nation's first foreign minister. From 2006 to 2007 he served as

Prime Minister, and from 2007 to 2012 he served as President. He was inaugurated as President for a second time on 20 May 2022, which was the 20th anniversary of the restoration of Timor-Leste's independence.

Greg Jericho is the Chief Economist at The Australia Institute and Centre for Future Work. He holds an Honours Degree in Economics from Flinders University. Greg also writes a weekly column on economics and politics for the *Guardian* Australia — a position he has held since 2013. In 2016 he won the Walkley Award for Commentary, Analysis, Opinion and Critique. Prior to working at The Australia Institute, Greg lectured in journalism and political communication at the University of Canberra and from 2006 to 2011 he worked in the Australian public service predominantly in the arts and film portfolios. In 2012 his book *The Rise of the Fifth Estate: Social Media and Blogging in Australian Politics* was published by Scribe.

Alana Johnson AM is a change specialist in the political, community, environment and agriculture sectors. Appointed a Member of the Order of Australia for services to women, Alana was inducted onto the Victorian Honour Roll of Women, and is Chair of the Victorian Women's Trust. A founder and past President of the acclaimed democracy group Voices for Indi, Alana is a founding Director and Convenor of the nationwide Community Independents Project and an author of *The Indi Way*. Alana is a recipient of a Distinguished Alumni Award from La Trobe University, and a fellow of the Australian Rural Leadership Foundation.

The Hon Michael Kirby was appointed a judicial officer in 1975. He served as inaugural Chairman of the Australian Law Reform Commission (1975–84); Judge of the Federal Court of Australia

(1983–4); President of the NSW Court of Appeal (1984–96); President, Court of Appeal Solomon Islands (1985–6) and Justice of the High Court of Australia (1996–2009). He also served on various UN bodies concerned with human rights including the COI on North Korea (2013–14). He has engaged with civil society, universities and other civil institutions. He was present at the launch of The Australia Institute in 1994 and returns for the 30th anniversary.

John Langmore is a Professorial Fellow in the School of Social and Political Sciences in the University of Melbourne. He has been a public servant and academic in Papua New Guinea; economic advisor to the Australian Treasurer; a Labor Member of the House of Representatives for 12 years; and a Divisional Director in the United Nations system in New York for seven years. At present he is working on the establishment of the Initiative for Peacebuilding at the University of Melbourne.

Thomas Mayo is a Torres Strait Islander man born on Larrakia country in Darwin. He was a wharf labourer before becoming a union official for the Maritime Union of Australia in his early thirties. He applied skills from the union movement to advancing the rights of Indigenous peoples, becoming a signatory to the Uluru Statement from the Heart. Following the Uluru Convention, Thomas was entrusted to carry the sacred canvas of the Uluru Statement from the Heart and embarked on an 18-month journey around the country to garner support for a constitutionally enshrined First Nations Voice, and a Makarrata Commission for truth-telling and agreement-making. Thomas is the author of five books for adults and children.

Professor Patrick McGorry AO is a psychiatrist known worldwide for his development and scaling up of early intervention and youth mental health services and for mental health innovation, advocacy and reform. He is Professor of Youth Mental Health at the University of Melbourne, and founding editor of the journal *Early Intervention in Psychiatry*. He has played a key advocacy and advisory role to government and health system reform in Australia and in many parts of the world. In 2010 Professor McGorry was selected as Australian of the Year and became an Officer of the Order of Australia. In 2016 he became the first psychiatrist to be elected as a Fellow of the Australian Academy of Science.

John McKinnon has a PhD in Social Enterprise and Development. He spent 17 years in the finance industry before joining overseas aid and development NGO, TEAR Australia, in 2005, managing first their NSW and then the Australian operations. John currently manages a charitable foundation and is involved with numerous NGOs, with both an environmental and anti-poverty focus.

Sally McManus was elected as Secretary of the ACTU in 2017, the first woman to hold this position since the creation of the ACTU in 1927. Sally has had a range of jobs; from a pizza deliverer to a cleaner while studying for her degree in Philosophy where she achieved First Class Honours and was also the President of the University Union. The *AFR* Power List has voted Sally as the fourth most powerful person in Australia in recognition of the role she holds and her leadership of the ACTU.

Christine Milne AO is a lifelong environmental, social justice and democracy advocate. Arrested and jailed in the campaign to save the Franklin River in 1983, she led the campaign to stop a native forest based, polluting pulp mill at Wesley Vale. Elected to the Tasmanian Parliament in 1989, she became the first female leader of a political party in Tasmania and went on to be elected to the Australian Senate 2005–15 and leader of the Australian Greens, 2012–15. She held the balance of power with the Tasmanian Field Labor and Rundle Liberal minority governments and the federal Gillard minority Labor government 2010–13. She has been part of the evolution of the Greens nationally and globally and is currently a Global Greens Ambassador.

Sunita Narain is an environmentalist and writer, and presently serves as the Director-General of Centre for Science and Environment (CSE) and Editor of the fortnightly magazine, *Down to Earth*. Dr Narain plays an active role in policy formulation on issues of environment and development in India and globally. She has co-authored influential publications on India's environment, conducted in-depth research on the governance and management of the country's environment and directed campaigns on air pollution control, community water management, sustainable industrialisation and food and toxins, among others. In 2016, she was featured in *Time* magazine's list of 100 Most Influential People in the World.

Karrina Nolan is a descendant of the Yorta Yorta people and an experienced manager and organiser of complex programs in Aboriginal communities. She has worked as a facilitator, trainer, researcher and strategist alongside First Nations communities for over 25 years. Most recently, Karrina has been building the capacity for self-determination in the context of economic development, climate change and clean energy. She has received Atlantic and Churchill fellowships.

Melissa Parke is Executive Director of the International Campaign to Abolish Nuclear Weapons. Melissa is a former Australian Minister for International Development and former Member of Parliament for the Australian Labor Party for Fremantle from 2007 to 2016. She began working on nuclear issues in the 1990s when she joined a campaign to oppose the establishment of a global nuclear waste dump in her home state of Western Australia. Prior to entering the Australian Parliament, Ms Parke served as an international lawyer with the United Nations in Kosovo, Gaza, New York and Lebanon. More recently, she served as a member of the UN Group of Eminent Experts on Yemen.

Kieran Pender is an associate legal director at the Human Rights Law Centre, where he leads the Whistleblower Project, Australia's first specialist legal service for whistleblowers. Kieran is also an honorary senior lecturer at the Australian National University College of Law, and an award-winning writer for the *Guardian*.

Amy Remeikis is a political journalist, author and commentator who covered Parliament for the *Guardian* Australia and regularly appears on ABC radio and TV and *The Project* on Channel Ten. She is Chief Political Strategist at The Australia Institute.

Jennifer Robinson is an award-winning Australian barrister at Doughty Street Chambers in London, specialising in human rights, media law, public law and international law. She has appeared in international, regional and domestic courts in key cases involving freedom of speech, human rights and climate change — and is renowned for successfully taking on powerful interests to tackle injustice. Her clients include journalists, media organisations, high-profile individuals, human rights defenders, governments and non-governmental organisations. The common thread of her career has been helping those who have the courage to stand up and speak out for what is right.

Brian Schmidt AC FAA FRS FTSE is Distinguished Professor of Astronomy at the ANU. For his work on the accelerating universe, Schmidt was awarded the 2011 Nobel Prize in Physics, jointly with Adam Riess and Saul Perlmutter. Schmidt has worked across many areas of astronomy including supernovae, gamma-ray bursts, gravitational wave transients, exo-planets, and metal poor stars. Receiving his PhD from Harvard University in 1993, Schmidt joined the staff of the Australian National University in 1995. He served as the 12th Vice-Chancellor and President of the ANU 2016 to 2023.

Dr Emma Shortis is Director of the International & Security Affairs Program at The Australia Institute. Emma is a historian and writer, focused on the history and politics of the United States and its role in the world. Emma's first book, *Our Exceptional Friend: Australia's Fatal Alliance with the United States*, was published by Hardie Grant in 2021. Before joining The Australia Institute, Emma was a Lecturer at RMIT University, where her academic work focused on international relations and climate transition. Before that, she spent a year in the United States as Fox-Zucker International Fellow at Yale University, where she finished her PhD in History.

Alex Sloan AM is an award-winning journalist and highly regarded interviewer, facilitator and MC. Alex has been a journalist for over 30 years, including 27 years as a broadcaster with the ABC. In 2017, Alex was named ACT Citizen of the Year, and in 2019 was appointed a Member of the Order of Australia.

Anna Spargo-Ryan is a Melbourne author, scriptwriter and editor. She has a PhD from Deakin University on the value of non-clinical language to transform mental health care. Her latest book, *A Kind of Magic*, was shortlisted in the Queensland Literary Awards.

Professor Fiona Stanley AC FAA FASSA FAHMS is founding Director and Patron, Telethon Kids Institute; Distinguished Research Professor, UWA; Honorary Professorial Fellow, University of Melbourne; UNICEF Ambassador for early childhood and Scientific Advisor, Doctors for the Environment. She trained overseas in Epidemiology and Maternal and Child Health, established population datasets in Western Australia including registers of major childhood problems, championed record linkage, and pioneered First Nations leadership in research. For her research on behalf of Australia's children and Aboriginal social justice, she was named Australian of the Year in 2003.

His Excellency Anote Tong is the former President of Kiribati, where he held office from 2003 to 2016. He is a decorated climate advocate, current chair of the Pacific Elders Voice (PEV) group and a former Board Member and Distinguished Fellow of Conservation International. He has been awarded the SunHak Peace Prize and has been twice nominated for the Nobel Peace Prize. He currently holds the Edmund Hillary Award and the Peter Benchley Ocean Award, as well as others, for his work on climate change and ocean conservation.

Lucy Hughes Turnbull AO is an urbanist, businesswoman and philanthropist. She has a particular interest in improving urban governance through collaboration across all government agencies — state and local — which, when it works, can deliver productive, sustainable and livable communities. She was the City of Sydney's first female Lord Mayor and Deputy Lord Mayor (1999–2004), a member and Chair of the Committee for Sydney (2004–15) and inaugural Chair of the Greater Sydney Commission (2015–20). She has also served on the board of many cultural institutions including the MCA, the Art Gallery of NSW and the Sydney Opera House Trust.

Yanis Varoufakis is an economist, political leader and the author of numerous bestselling books: *Technofeudalism*; *Talking to My Daughter: A Brief History of Capitalism*; *Adults in the Room*, a memoir of his time as finance minister of Greece; an economic history of Europe, *And The Weak Suffer What They Must?*; and *Another Now: Dispatches from An Alternative Present*. Born in Athens in 1961, he was for many years a professor of economics in Britain, Australia and the US before he entered politics. He is co-founder of the international grassroots movement DiEM25 and a Professor of Economics at the University of Athens.

Professor Clare Wright OAM is an award-winning historian, author, broadcaster, podcaster and public commentator. Clare is Professor of History and Professor of Public Engagement at La Trobe University. She is the author of five books, including the bestselling and Stella Prize-winning *The Forgotten Rebels of Eureka*. Clare has written and presented documentaries for ABC TV, hosts the RN podcast *Shooting the Past*, co-hosts the podcast *Archive Fever* (with Yves Rees) and is Executive Producer of *Hey History!* the first Australian history podcast designed for the classroom. In 2020, Clare was awarded a Medal of the Order of Australia for "services to literature and to historical research". Clare is Chair of the National Museum of Australia Council and past Board Director of the Wheeler Centre for Books, Writing and Ideas.

Acknowledgements

The Australia Institute was founded on Ngunnawal and Ngambri country, and we acknowledge the unbroken connection to and care for country that First Nations people have had for tens of millennia.

Since its inception over 30 years ago, the work of numerous staff, board, contributors, volunteers and friends of the Institute — those who have worked at The Australia Institute and those who have been gracious in lending their time, ideas, or even just their names — has built the organisation into the leading think tank it is today.

Our thanks also go to all the incredible contributors who have been generous enough to take the time to put their big idea on paper. This book is more than the sum of its parts because of the way your ideas form a roadmap for potential change. Thank you for these essays that together create a book worth celebrating.

Our heartfelt thanks to the thousands of wonderful people who have donated to The Australia Institute to make all this work possible. We do not accept donations from political parties and are entirely independent — proudly so. We can only do what we do because of supporters like you. Big or small, your contributions have not only made our last 30 years of work possible, but will power our next 30 years of work to create an Australia full of possibility. Thank you.

This book is a celebration of The Australia Institute's
30th anniversary — 30 years of big ideas.

Becoming a monthly donor safeguards our work as we bring big ideas to life. Every dollar you donate will power research that matters and help make these big ideas a reality.

It takes a team. When you donate to The Australia Institute you are supporting our team of researchers and experts to improve public policy. It is people like you who make The Australia Institute's research impact possible.

Visit australiainstitute.org.au, or scan the QR code below, to donate today.

Support The Australia Institute